# SYSTEMATIC THEOLOGY

# Systematic Theology
## (Dogmatik)

BY

## WILHELM HERRMANN

TRANSLATED BY

### NATHANIEL MICKLEM, M.A.
OF THE SELLY OAK COLLEGES, BIRMINGHAM

AND

### KENNETH A. SAUNDERS, M.A., B.Litt.
OF SOLIHULL

WIPF & STOCK · Eugene, Oregon

Wipf and Stock Publishers
199 W 8th Ave, Suite 3
Eugene, OR 97401

Systematic Theology (Dogmatik)
By Herrmann, Wilhelm and Micklem, Nathaniel
ISBN 13: 978-1-62564-033-8
Publication date 4/15/2013
Previously published by Macmillan, 1927

# TRANSLATORS' FOREWORD

For a generation Dr. Wilhelm Herrmann was one of the most influential and respected of the religious teachers of Britain as well as of Germany; for not only was his great book, *The Communion of the Christian with God,* widely known here in translation, but he was the most outstanding figure of the Ritschlian school which has profoundly affected British thinking. Marburg, where Herrmann taught, became before the war something like a place of pilgrimage for younger theologians from the British universities. Herrmann was a fine scholar, but his teaching was marked by a moving religious and indeed prophetic fervor, and even his lectures had an evangelical quality.

This present volume was published in Germany after his death; it was never prepared by him for the press, nor intended to be a book. It was his habit when lecturing to dictate a paragraph to his audience and then to expatiate upon it *ex tempore.* This book contains what appears to be the final, or best, form of his constantly revised paragraphs for dictation. It is therefore very closely knit in form and gives the finest essence only of his message.

Of his life there is not much that need be said; he was born on December 6, 1846, a son of the Manse.

In 1866 he went to the University of Halle. His philosophical ability impressed Professor Ulrichi, who sought to divert him from theology to philosophy. But Herrmann's heart was in theology, even though in Halle he found the theological atmosphere most uncongenial. It was to Albrecht Ritschl, of Bonn, that he gave his allegiance, and Ritschl's influence that dominated his mind. In 1879 he went to Marburg as professor, and from Marburg till his death on January 2, 1922, he exercised a personal and theological and spiritual ministry which has profoundly influenced modern Protestantism .

It is hoped that the appearance of this book in English may be of wide usefulness and advantage to the Protestant Churches. The translators desire to thank the publisher for his patience and the Rev. Norman Robinson, M.A., of Moseley, for his careful and valuable revision of their manuscript.

N. M.
K. A. S.

BIRMINGHAM.
       May, 1926.

# CONTENTS

## PART I

## RELIGION

9

# CONTENTS

### SECTION II

*The Overcoming of Sin through Faith which is God's Gift.*

*PART I*

# RELIGION

# Systematic Theology

## CHAPTER I

## THE SCIENCE OF RELIGION

1. *The general task of the science of religion.*

As soon as a religious community seeks to assert itself within a growing intellectual culture, it requires a science of the religion it represents. To this end religion must try to prove itself over against the other intellectual forces of culture as a power which is stronger than all of them; for this, however, it is necessary to show that in it, too, there is something of universal validity which can win recognition by intellectual means. The examination of this question and the elaboration of such a proof is the task of the science or, as it is often called, the philosophy of religion. We hold this to be—not indeed the whole task, but certainly the first task of a Christian systematic theology. For the Christian community needs to solve this question in its own interest, since it desires not to separate itself from culture, but in every faithful Christian man to permeate culture with the power of true religion; it is necessary, too, in the interests of the individual Christian, that he may become conscious of that which may rank as universally valid (objective) knowledge.

Besides this, the Christian community sets another task to the science of religion. The distinctive quality of the Christian religion or the basis and content of faith must be set forth. This, however, would be impossible if the first task had not already been disposed of, and if that which can alone be reckoned as universally valid in religion had not been more exactly defined than is usually the case. Only on this basis can that which is distinctive in the Christian religion be appraised in its proper greatness. This is connected with the third task of the science of religion, which is to interpret the ideas that arise in religion in the light of this their origin.

The branch of theology which is charged with these three tasks is to-day generally called "Dogmatics." [1] This name arose among Protestants about the end of the seventeenth century, but it is to be explained as a relic of Catholicism; for with us there cannot be a systematic but only a historical science of dogma, since Evangelical Christianity cannot have any dogmas in the old sense of the term. Dogma in that sense corresponds only with the type of religion represented by Judaism or the Roman Church.

If we retain, then, the name "dogmatics," it is only because, as in the older dogmatics, we desire to explicate both the foundations and the content of the Christian faith, and there is no point in unnecessarily abandoning a familiar term.

2. *The hidden nature of religion.*

The scientific investigation of religion has to meet a difficulty which we do not find in the inquiries of

---

[1] The title of this book in German is *Dogmatik.*

natural science and ethics. Everybody can be convinced by demonstration that there is such a thing as science or knowledge that advances with sure steps—such a thing also as a volition or a morality of universal validity. Mankind therefore finds common ground in a culture which is based on the universal validity of science and morality. We may count on general understanding when we speak of those kinds of spiritual activity. Even the sceptic involuntarily assumes this culture, in the act of contesting it. Therefore if we want to examine science and morality in relation to truth, we have to deal with thoughts which are the common property of every man capable of thinking; we can count on the object of investigation being known by all. In the case of religion we cannot assume the same common knowledge. The possession of religion is not an essential element in human life in the same way as are knowledge and will, when they appear in logical form as science and morality. Religion is not something so objectively real that it must needs be observed by all; it appears only in individuals as a spiritual possession, as something peculiar. This accounts for the fact that there are many people who not only maintain that they themselves are strangers to religion, but also suspect that what others say about it rests upon self-deception. They do not regard religion as a reality. On the other hand, the man who can see and understand religion as a reality knows that this is due to the influence of those experiences in which he has personal and living consciousness of religion. Thus every man's attitude to religion and his idea of it is relative to his individual life. If this is true, it seems impossible in the case of a science of religion to ask for what is of universal validity; on any other terms the science of religion itself seems to be impossible. (Luke xvii. 21; Matt. xiii. 11; John xviii. 36; 1 Cor. ii. 1, 7 and 10.)

3. *The possibility of a science of religion.*

If the science of religion deals with a reality which can be grasped only by certain people, then it must, of course, renounce that claim to universal acknowledgment which the natural sciences can make good. It can claim the name of real knowledge only from such men as are gifted with special experiences, and in whom in consequence a new life has arisen.

This does not prove its worthlessness as science, but it shows that its object, religion itself, belongs to history and not to nature. History as a whole cannot compel the recognition of its data, because that which is strictly called historical can be perceived as a reality only by those who in some way experience it. We can understand a personality in its reality only by having something of its life alive in our own spiritual life; or at least we must be capable of the desire to follow it or to fight against it. The same is true of religion; wherefore the science of religion is to be cognized by the same means as the science of history in general—not by the formulation of rules, but by the representation of a reality in which a man's own experience participates. We have to describe religion as we can see it—first in ourselves, and then (and only then) in others. A man, however, who has no personal experience of religion, cannot be convinced of it by the science of religion; as little can the heroes of history be made convincing to the man who is wallowing in sensuality. They will only be visible to him in those moments when he is mourning his own weakness and longing for liberation.

Nevertheless, the science of religion can be of service also to the man who is as yet devoid of any personal experience of religion. If it cannot set him face to face with the reality of religion, it can at least put him on the way to it. It can do him this service, however, only as his own unrecognized craving for religion emerges into consciousness. To make this clear is the first task of the science of religion. A second task arises from the importance of the religious community for the life of religion. Religion may be awakened in different people by the action upon them of the same fact. These people are then bound together, by an experience determining their whole life, into a religious community. It is for the science of religion in every such community to make clear and defend from distortion the religious experience of its members, and the expression of religion common to them all.

Work on the first task can claim universal validity in the same degree as the science of history in general. Work on the second task, though not entirely confined to the circle of a definite religious community, is none the less understandable only by those who share the experience of religion, even though it be in another form.

## CHAPTER II

## THE INTELLECTUAL APPREHENSION
## OF RELIGION

4. *The basic general idea of religion.*

We must first of all posit that which the religiously minded man clearly perceives to be the vital thing in everything which impresses him as showing the essential characteristics of religion. This general idea of religion, which is obvious to every religiously minded man without any profound investigation, runs as follows: To every religiously minded man religion means seeing the working of a God in the events of life. The more exact explication of this spiritual fact is our scientific task. We shall fulfil this task by observing how religion is sought in man's life, how it arises in ourselves, and how it works itself out in thought and action.

5. *Contradictory valuations of religion.*

In the scientific treatment of religion we meet first of all the contradiction between its positive valuation as our supreme spiritual possession and its disparagement as pure illusion. Even in the former case where one seeks in religion the fulfilment of life, two views of its essence stand opposed to each other. The "intellectualist" explanation is widely held. According to this view it is held to be always possible to reduce religion to something else, as it is our task to do in the fathoming of all phenomena. The opposite point of view is that presented to us in the Scriptures —the religious conception of religion which regards it as irreducible to anything else, and as simply a wonderful fact apprehensible only by those who are endowed with it. Let us attempt first an analysis of the former—the intellectualist—conception.

6. *The attempt to base religion upon the scientific knowledge of the world.*

In the story of religion we find the idea that the world actually proves to men the existence of God (Rom. i. 19–20, and many passages in the Psalter). If God is to us really the Lord over all, then we shall expect to find the traces of his Lordship in all things. It has, however, for a long time escaped notice that this thought arises out of religion itself and is impotent and groundless divorced from its source. So long as knowledge of God was regarded independent of religion, it was thought possible to find religion along this path. From the reality of the world which science can investigate the attempt was made so to demonstrate the reality of God as to compel the assent of every thinking man. All such proofs are scientifically untenable, and the idea that a man can come to religion in this way is inconsistent with its essential nature.

Of all these attempts only the cosmological proof deserves serious refutation; for that really contains a right and highly scientific notion. The teleological proof, on the contrary, is scientifically a quite indefensible attempt to find a basis upon which to prove the existence of God; it cannot claim any scientific value whatever. The teleological proof seeks to prove from the observed purposiveness in nature that a purposive Spirit is the creator of this world. The Spirit whose existence is thus arrived at must clearly (the argument proceeds) be the God of religious faith. Thus is faith demonstrated, as regards its most important conception, to be a matter of scientifically grounded knowledge. But, in the first place, we do not know the totality of things. Parts of an unlimited reality are all we ever know. In the second place, we do not by any means always find in the world, as we know it, a purposeful order. Rather we are often oppressed with a sense of meaningless events. It is just here that the distinctive power of religion should be manifested, in giving to man the power to resolve this perplexity and in face of these impressions to maintain the conviction that wisdom rules the universe. In the third place, even if this argument were sound, it would prove the existence not of God, i.e. a Being of absolute wisdom and power, but only of a Being of wisdom and power higher than our own. The wonderful purposiveness of nature is indeed of high value for the life of religion, reminding the religious man as it does of the riches of his God, and unveiling to all men the inscrutable nature of reality. But as a basis for religion the teleological argument is entirely worthless.

The cosmological proof starts from the fact that

everything to which we can point is conditioned by other things. Had we, however, to imagine all things as thus conditioned, we should be unable in the end to ascribe existence in the full sense to anything whatsoever. We must therefore conceive the notion of a Reality distinct from this world, a Reality self-existent or absolute, on which all finite things depend, and from which they derive their share of reality. With the thought of this absolute Reality we should obviously have arrived at the thought of God Almighty. Now it is perfectly true that science can only securely grasp the reality of things in time and space when they can be conceived in relation to an eternal Being. But in the work of science the eternal ground of all being is, as a matter of fact, never expressed in terms of God, but always in the conception of law. In the attempt to substantiate the reality of a thing, the way of science is always to seek to make good the proposition that this thing is bound up with all other things in one uniform nature. The idea underlying this hypothesis—that of an all-embracing law—is that which for science expresses the eternal ground of all that is in time and space.

### 7. *The reduction of religion to the life-force of the individual.*

Outside of the Roman Church confidence in proofs for the existence of God is gone. On the other hand, many people suppose that men could be brought to religion by demonstrating its origin in the essential nature of the spirit of man, in his life-force.

Amongst the present-day sponsors of this attempt

Julius Kaftan amongst theologians and Rudolf Eucken amongst philosophers deserve special attention. Kaftan explains religion as a practical concern of the spirit, as something, that is to say, which it fundamentally needs. The right way to understand the nature of religion is to track down the motives of this fundamental impulse. He argues that religion reaches out in two directions. It seeks, on the one hand, by the aid of a transcendent Power to arrive at the truth of human life; it strives, on the other hand, after redemption from the world through participation in divine life. Since, then, both tendencies are directed towards a perfect life or the supreme good, one may most simply define religion as that form of spiritual life which is marked by its direction towards a supreme good. Thus the essence of religion is the desire for the fulfilment of life by means of a transcendent Power; the desire for the fulfilment of life is obviously at work in the whole life of man as it unfolds itself in history. Religion indeed is vindicated as true, if it can be demonstrated that it really leads man to satisfaction. Such a demonstration is possible in the case of Christianity alone.

Eucken has not attained to the clarity and simplicity of Kaftan's exegesis. In his writings he is always trying to show that man's striving after a real, and therefore distinct, personal life is perfectly realized only in religion. But the truth, or the justification, of religion is not found by Eucken in its significance for the fulfilment of life; he thinks he can prove, by the manner in which the motives of religion come to dominate life, the actual influence of a reality distinct from nature, "a higher world." That there is a reality, a home of the soul, distinct from nature, he seeks to prove from the fact, manifested in history, of life reaching its climax in religion. From this fact would follow the truth of that idea which constitutes the content of religion. ⌐The fact of religion must itself guarantee the truth of its ideas. But a living religious conviction alone will see in religion anything more than the creation of human cravings. Eucken's expositions suffer from confusion in that he always employs ideas, which are an expression of religious conviction already there, to describe facts by which religious conviction is to be established.

None the less, this very mistake of Eucken's itself registers an advance on Kaftan; Eucken has seen that religion is in great jeopardy if its essence, as with Kaftan, is to be defined by an unveiling of its motives. If religion is based on the desire to win and assure the goal of life, it is exposed to a serious objection. It may be said that its wonderful conceptions, giving the lie, as they do, to what forces itself on the human mind as indisputably real, are simply the expression of what man desires to have. In that case religion cannot escape the suspicion that its ideas, though beautiful, are not true. It is precisely in this way that religion has been conceived by its most determined opponents: in the eighteenth century by Hume, in the nineteenth by Feuerbach. Religion which could be really understood as the product of our own life-force would be thereby not vindicated but condemned. Eucken tries to avoid this danger. The vogue, however, which he enjoys is due to the fact that he deals with religion as a philosopher, and as such expresses a forceful point of view in regard to the religious life. For many feel their minds made easy when a "philosopher" enters the list on behalf of a scientific proof of the rights of religion. But a proof with so serious a logical defect is bound in the end to injure the cause which it sets out to defend.

## 8. *The derivation of religion from the moral will.*

Kant thought that religion had its origin in moral earnestness. To possess religion is man's duty; for though the bent towards religion is not a natural instinct implanted in every living man, one could easily demonstrate to morally serious people their own innate demand for religion. Kant rightly perceived that man, in the moment when he is willing to deny himself in the service of good, must be filled with the conviction that the good is the absolute power. For the determination to let the good reign in us would not take shape unless we found it possible to think of the good will as all-powerful. As long as our consciousness clings to the idea that something else may be as powerful as the good, so long is our consciousness incompletely swayed by it. Consequently, in the moment of ethical action, when a man is in the grip of moral conviction, he conceives of the good will as the sovereign power in the universe. Kant is also quite right in observing that this idea of the power of the good will belongs to religion. But his inference that a man possesses religion if he is filled with a sense of the truth of this notion is not correct. It is only true that religion and morality can meet in these conceptions. On the other hand, it is possible to perceive the truth of this notion without having any religion. For while it is true that the strength of ethical insight finds expression in the idea of the power of the good, yet, though real religion always carries with it such a power and recognizes itself as a particular mode of its activity, it does not grow out of the ethical will alone.

Kant contributed to the emancipation of religion by severing it from its perilous connection with the knowledge of empirical reality (i.e. with science). But he failed to present religion in its independent and underivable essence. For it was hidden from him that religion contains something which distinguishes it from ethical will, although it is always bound up with morality, or strives to identify itself with the will. He would quite approve the claim of the modern Kantians that religion resolves itself into morality, because its truth is nothing but ethical insight. Schleiermacher, in the days of his youth, attempted to correct this mistake of Kant; but in the final form of his theory of religion he fell short of the point which Kant reached, for he ultimately lost Kant's great intuition that religion is only to be found in the man who addresses himself to action,' or, in other words, in the life of man regarded from the historical and not the merely naturalistic standpoint. "Ethics leads inevitably to religion, whereby it develops into the idea of a puissant ethical Law-giver outside the individual. In the will of this Law-giver is found the final goal which can and must be man's chief end."[1]

[1] *Religion Within the Limits of Pure Reason.*

9. *The reduction of religion to the unity of self-con-
    sciousness.*[1]

Schleiermacher in sections 3–5 of his *Glaubenslehre*
and in his *Dialektik* did not intend to explain the
origin of religion from a single motive, but to deduce
its reality from the unity of self-consciousness. Even
this foundation, however, is not tenable. It may be
expected *a priori* that what is to be found in every
consciousness cannot be religion itself, but at best
a condition for the possibility of religion.

Schleiermacher refers to the fact that we can perceive in ourselves another form of consciousness
besides that knowing and willing with which we address
ourselves to definite objects. In "feeling" consciousness finds itself in a condition in which it does not
yet distinguish particular objects from itself; in a
vague emotion it recognizes the dawning of reality.
In such a moment it is our experience that we are
not partly dependent on things and partly in control
of them as in knowing and in action; we observe
rather that we are in the last resort absolutely dependent. For without our co-operation and irrespective
of what we wish, the stimuli to new ideas of real
things or to new endeavors of the will arise from
depths unknown to us and press upon us. We perceive ourselves, then, to be obviously in the grip of a
power irresistible and inexorable. The consciousness
of this situation, or this "feeling," which may, beyond
doubt, be awakened in every man, is, then, according

[1] In 1915: The attempt to prove religion an element in every
human consciousness.

to Schleiermacher, the proper essence of religion. He thinks that it is reducible to this sense of absolute dependence in which consciousness first comes to expression, and that the power of religion becomes intelligible as coming from this source.

But that which Schleiermacher emphasizes as being undoubtedly present in consciousness is no more than the outcome of the fact that our existence is entirely dependent on unknown powers. The comprehension of this fact, however, in no way implies religion. This conciousness is certainly a condition of the first stirring of religion; it is also a factor in the developed life of religion; but it does not in itself constitute religion. Moreover, that incomprehensible power over our existence is not the God of religious faith. For this power is visible to the atheist too, if he thinks on the infinitude of reality, with the regular processes of which our existence is bound up. Its name is therefore fate, not God.

# CHAPTER III

## THE FOUNDATION OF THE SCIENCE OF RELIGION IN THE HISTORICAL FACT OF RELIGION

10. *Religion as historical fact.*

Before Schleiermacher formed the untenable theory of the essence of religion which aimed at demonstrating it to be a constituent part of every consciousness, he had in his earlier work, his addresses "On Religion," developed quite a different conception, which, in spite of its violent polemics against Kant, betrays the characteristic quality of Kantian thought. He does not here treat religion as a demonstrable trait in all human consciousness, but as a historical phenomenon which is to be seen in actual existence only in individuals. · He repudiates the notion of Rationalism that historical forms must be derived from natural religion. By so doing he also avoids the mistaken idea of the modern historians of religion that religion may be known from the fullest possible observation of it in others. Religion can only be perceived in others by the man who already knows from his own experience what religion is. Schleiermacher's presentation of religion is, therefore, based on two facts—his knowledge of it as a real and active factor in history, and his own personal experience of it. His view of religion is the expression of his own religion.

Schleiermacher addresses himself to the cultured. By the cultured he means people who take morality seriously. He was thus, at that time, at one with Kant in supposing that moral obedience is the only way to religion. He told the seriously minded people that if they despised religion they had a conception of it undeserving of the name, and they had no inkling of the fact that real religion is just that spiritual liberation which they themselves desired. If, like them, one were to give to a kind of shackled science and chained morality the name of religion, one would be perfectly right in despising it. But science is something quite different from religion. Science sets out to prove the reality of things as a system of natural law; religion makes no such attempt. Religion, on the contrary, posits a reality which to the man who sees it seems a miracle—a miracle that he himself can experience but can demonstrate to no one else. No less clear is the distinction between morality and religion. In morality man must not obey an alien will, but his own sense of absolute obligation, which is the moral end of volition. Morality means always independence, whereas in religion man feels himself in the power of a Being to whom he surrenders himself. It means sheer dependence. Therefore science and morality masquerading as religion would be untrue to themselves and merit contempt. Both have to base themselves on that which every man can recognize as universally valid. On the other hand, the peculiarity of religion consists in the very fact that it cannot be reduced to the knowledge of something universally valid, but simply to that secret life of the soul which the individual alone can recognize in each case as a reality. It must, therefore, have in everyone its own special history; there is no religion which can be identical in all men; religion exists only in individuals.

The content of religion which thus exists in individuals and groups is called by Schleiermacher an individually determined conception of the universe. This has often been understood in a pantheistic sense. But Schleiermacher meant by it that the essential content of religion does not consist in any kind of ideas of transcendent things; its essence is rather a particular way in which man experiences the whole of reality; he possesses religion when this reality, which first of all appears to all men as an indefinite plurality, becomes for him an ordered whole or a universe. This happens when a man perceives in reality the unity of an inexhaustible life. Schleiermacher thus implies that religion means to grasp as real a transcendent Entity. For the Being who thus gives unity to the world is not an inference from the actual constitution of the world; yet if we are in a position to perceive in everything the expression of one hidden life, we have a transcendent element in the unity of the real thus implied.

If this correctly states the essence of religion, then that man is irreligious for whom reality is dumb and senseless or dead; to him ordinary life has nothing to say; on the contrary, he hankers after something extraordinary. But he is the religious man who, in every experience which moves his spirit, hears a single, living Power speak to his soul. The strongest and purest piety will be that of the man who, in *every* experience that quickens him within, recognizes the language of a love that seeks his response. To experience all events as the work of such a Being, and to recognize as the principle of the universe the love which makes for independent life—this is perfect religion. Schleiermacher here gives expression to the complete consciousness of religion in the language of science; by this we mean that he makes clear the distinction between religion and the other chief forms of the life of the spirit—science, morality and art.

11. *The way to religion.*

Religion can be understood only by the man who himself lives in it. But the way to religion may be shown to anyone who does not repudiate moral obligation.

We are continually possessed by the idea that we enjoy an independent life. At the same time the fact forces itself inexorably upon us in ever new forms that we have no life that is really such; the consequence is that the real life we would fain claim becomes a mere semblance; our life becomes an empty thing. This is, of course, bearable to all those who make no attempt to unify their personality. A man only comes to inward unity when he sets his heart upon a cause which he serves; in other words, he must be a man who really works; therefore religion also is attained only by the burden-bearers of mankind— by those, that is to say, who work for others. Such men, so long as they do not lose themselves down by-paths, can never get quit of the task of attaining a real unification of their inner life. This is for them an inexorable moral demand. But when they earnestly seek to meet it, they come to recognize as never before that, while they always have before their eyes the goal of inward independence or true life, yet they never attain it. Moral seriousness, therefore, will intensify but not solve the question of how this consciousness of possessing an inner life of our own, which haunts us continually, can be reconciled with reality.

The consciousness of having a life of our own can be justified neither by science nor by ethics. But moral earnestness will not allow us to escape the question of how the idea of a self can be reconciled with reality; and if this idea cannot be substantiated by universally valid conceptions of science and ethics, the only possibility remaining is that, in order to discover the reality of our life, we fall back upon that which we can neither establish for others nor share with them. It may still be possible for us, out of our own individual and private experience, to find our way to a real life for ourselves. This is a question that must arise in the mind of everyone who finds it intolerable to live a life devoid of reality. And here, for the cultured man of to-day, lies the way to religion.

12. *The basis which religion finds for itself in the experience of revelation.*

The experiences out of which man acquires the power of real life or becomes religious are called by religion itself "revelations." Such experiences can come only to the man who has been shaken and rendered desperate by the fact that his own life is without truth, and therefore impotent and null. In the longing to escape from this condition of despair, from the untruth of the idea (which sways his whole existence) that he has a life of his own—here lies for us the way to God.

But even then we cannot of ourselves achieve the discovery of God. Religion cannot exist without the exercise of the moral will, but it does not spring from this root. Revelation, which saves man, must be given to him as his most compelling experience. The content of this experience does not consist (as Schleiermacher thought) in our consciousness of absolute dependence. The experience of revelation must of course involve, for the very reason that it is necessarily a gift to us, the pure consciousness of an absolute dependence. But if in this instance we are to find real life, the experience must be likewise filled with the clear consciousness of our freedom or inward independence. We can only have an idea of this fundamental religious experience which we call revelation if we are able to recall a time when we knew a moment of utter dependence which was also an act of free will. We could not imagine such an experience, but we can recognize it when it is really there. We have it before our eyes at the moment when we know ourselves to be in the grip of a spiritual power which acts on us as the manifestation of pure goodness. For in the presence of this manifestation we find ourselves in fact in a condition of sheer voluntary dependence, of complete submission, which is at the same time a joyful revival of our own soul. The experience out of which religion may arise, then, is the realization on the part of any religious man that he has encountered a spiritual Power in contact with which he has felt utterly humbled, yet at the same time uplifted to a real independent inner life. This is met with in ordinary life, when in the society of our fellows we experience in ourselves the awakening of reverence and trust.

13. *The awakening of religion in obedience to revelation.*
If we have experienced the working of this Power, through contact with which a life which is life in truth, a real human life, arises in us, then we are in a position to settle the question whether God is a reality to us. It simply depends on whether we remain loyal to the truth, that is, whether we are prepared to treat the fact of such a Power as what it really is for us. The moment we desire dependence upon it, and submit ourselves to it in reverence and trust, this spiritual Power is really our soul's Lord. We can never again entirely forget the fact that we have met with a Power which had not only an external sway over us but subdued our hearts. In the moment of this experience we possess a life that is such in truth. We may, however, so disregard this fact that it is put into the shade by something else that monopolizes our interest. If this occurs, then we are trying to hide from ourselves a fact which we are well aware has primary claims upon us. The outcome of such an unconscientious attitude of mind is to make religion

impossible.   For religion can arise only with the will
to truth, which puts all other considerations on one
side.   We can only be truthful if we are prepared to
treat that which has become an indubitable and
incomparably potent fact as what it really is.   If we
know that in certain moments we find ourselves in
the presence of a Power which inwardly constrains us,
we can only remain truthful by showing to this Power
the reverence which we know to be its due.   This
we do only when we refuse to close our eyes to the
implication, clearly marked in that very experience,
that this Power, in contact with which we attain
to real life, is itself living.   Nothing is so clear to us
as that what is dead can never give life to anyone.
Even ethical considerations cannot of themselves
give life (Gal. iii. 21).   But when repeatedly, in the
moments in which our life is filled with a new reality,
we perceive ourselves to be in the presence of the same
living Power, the first result is the conviction that
this Power is at work in all the movements of that
inner life which is its hidden realm.   We come to
look for the evidences of this Power in everything
that stirs our inner life.   Hence our daily experience gains such wealth and depth that we know ourselves to be transported into what, compared with
the common life of man, is a new existence.   The
second result is that we respond to this living Power
which thus makes itself perceptible to us, and constantly seek to understand its promptings in ethical
demand and in the varied experience of life.   In
this way religion comes to fruition in us and our life
becomes a life in truth, since we now have very dis-

tinctly before us the Reality to which we as living beings can belong.

Religion that arises in this way may obviously find its basis in two facts. First in individual recollections of human goodness which stand in contrast to experiences of an opposite kind. But the trust in God which would take its stand upon such recollections can assert itself only by thrusting into the background whatever contradicts them. Secondly, religion which finds its God in such recollections can appeal to the help which it brings to people in their distress. But even the religious man may for a long time be so little conscious of such help that he feels himself abandoned by his God. The religion of the Old Testament bears the marks of this stress of conflict between the consciousness of the claims of religion and the temptation wearily to abandon the fight in the face of doubt. But precisely in virtue of this characteristic of moral conflict, the religion of the Old Testament stands pre-eminent above all previous or contemporary religions. The faith of the New Testament bears beyond question the marks of a peace which the Old Testament lacks. This proves that the ground of its confidence is clearer and surer. If, however, this Christian faith is not to fall below the level of the Old Testament, it must also succeed in showing that it still retains the ethical character of an unflagging battle for life that is life indeed.

14. *The conception of revelation in the older theology.*

In our opinion nothing in religion should be called revelation save what is capable of setting us face to face with the reality of God, and can thus become the basis of religion in us. In earlier theology, however, we find as a rule three other points of view, the traditionalist, the rationalist, and the mystical. Each of these represents a very important religious conception, but all quite fail to express the very thing that religion looks for in revelation.

1. According to the traditionalist view revelation is a tradition which communicates to us the forms in which the faith of religious men once expressed itself. That this definition is not satisfactory follows from the fact that we can give the name of revelation only to that which is the foundation of our own faith. The way in which others have expressed their faith cannot possibly provide a foundation for our own faith. It does not help us in the least if we allow ourselves to be told that the content of religious conviction is furnished for us by tradition, and are then prepared to call this tradition revelation; for we have no religion at all till religious conviction is created in ourselves; and only that which effects this in us ranks for us as revelation. Real revelation does not merely tell us what others have believed; it makes us ourselves believers. Failure to grasp this is the defect of traditionalism. Its merit is the loyalty to religious tradition that will even honor tradition with the name of "revelation." It is right in its emphasis upon the fact that the revelation which helps man must be within the sphere of history, and must therefore find its expression in tradition.

2. *Rationalism* starts from the assumption that we can have religion only through our own knowledge

of God, and not through that of others. From this perfectly correct proposition it draws the conclusion that the idea of God must rise out of our own reason.

Religion can have truth only as it is conscious of its origin in necessary processes of thought. To the rationalists, therefore, reason itself ranks as the source of religion or as "revelation." But if the idea of God could be derived from man's own thinking, it would belong to his scientific knowledge. Religion, however, is not ours in such "knowledge"; we possess it only when we come to the consciousness that God is working upon us (in some particular situation) as the Power which saves us. It is to his personal experience of this that every religious man ascribes the vitality of his religion. Such experience cannot, however, be conceived as an "eternal truth" or as the product of our own reflection; those to whom it is granted can view it only as a wonderful fact. Traditionalism and rationalism, though usually at daggers drawn, are at one in this, that both look for revelation not in an experience of which the individual is actually conscious, but in notions which claim universal validity.

3. In distinction from these two conceptions the life of religion can really be expressed in the mystical conception. While in traditionalism it is not really the voice of religion that one hears but the voice of the ecclesiastical institution, and in rationalism of a "science" which has never made clear to itself the limits of its knowledge, mysticism at least recognizes that its revelation, in which religion must find its ground, must belong to the religious man's own life,

and must be experienced by him as a present reality. But mysticism has not satisfactorily defined this experience upon which living religion is based; for it describes it as a wonderful emotion which may arise in a man's soul without any connection with the experiences of life in the world. Therefore mysticism always tends to turn its back upon that real world in which man finds himself. The mystic seeks the way to God not in reflection on the actual facts of his own life, but in an emotion worked up by phantasy. The religion of the mystic arises out of a kind of religious technique. But a religion that has become conscious of such an origin can in no way fortify itself against doubt, once the emotion caused by phantasy ceases to have the power completely to suppress all question as to the truth of the religion.

On the other hand, the ground of a religion which sets itself this question can only be found in a revelation which a man distinguishes from his own life. Hence such a revelation can be sought only in that reality which we cannot gainsay, not in emotions and feelings which we seek to induce by turning our backs upon the reality that presses upon us. It is precisely in this inexorable reality that we must find the Power to which alone we can know ourselves entirely subject. If that is impossible, then religion itself is for us impossible.

# CHAPTER IV

# THE CHRISTIAN RELIGION

15. *The distinguishing mark of religion in the Christian community.*

When a man seeks God he is really seeking to apprehend that power on which he can feel himself to be in complete dependence.  If we are brought up in the Christian community, we obtain a notion of this primarily from our experience of the self-sacrificing love of Christians for us; but these men themselves give us to understand that it is to the Person of Jesus that they owe the power with which they influence us.  All that binds us to them is derived from the Person of Jesus and gives us reason to expect that what we all seek will be found more purely and potently under his direct influence than when mediated by those about us.  Hence, if we want to know how the distinctively Christian type of religion may become powerful in us we must—

1. Find out from the tradition preserved in the Christian community how the personality of Jesus impressed itself upon the memory of his first disciples;

2. We must then try to learn how he mediated to these people the experiences which became God's revelation to them;

3. We must ask ourselves how the Person of Jesus
can become for us such a present fact as to effect the
same in our case.

## 16. *The Kingdom of God which Jesus sought to establish.*

The Synoptists depict the work and fate of a man
who was convinced that the Kingdom of God was
coming through his own life and work. If we desire,
therefore, to understand the Jesus whom this tradition
depicts, in regard to his own conception of his mission
or in his inner life, we must first of all understand
what he meant by that Kingdom of God which was to
be realized through his life. We must start from two
established facts :—

1. Where Jesus lived this phrase stood for that which
was the hope of religious minds.

2. Jesus understood this expression in such a way as
to incur the enmity of the religious people of his day.

It follows from both facts that in the sayings of
Jesus conventional expressions may occur, which by
themselves do not perfectly represent his thoughts,
and must therefore be modified or amplified by other
sayings of his. Jesus must then have seen in the
Jewish conceptions of the "Kingdom of God" both
a means to his work and a hindrance to it.

Jesus agreed in two points with the conception
current among the Jews of his time: (1) he, like
them, understood by the Kingdom of God that which
should make men blessed (Matt. v. 10; vi. 33) ; a man
must therefore be ready to give up everything else for
the Kingdom of God (Matt. vi. 33; x. 37; xviii. 8) ;

(2) Jesus was in agreement with the religious belief of his contemporaries that the Kingdom of God cannot develop out of the present order or be realized through human activity, but that it comes down to earth from heaven by a miraculous act of God. The Kingdom of God comes from the other world. It is not the result of human activity, but a gift of God.

On the other hand, Jesus set himself in opposition to the religion of his compatriots first in his assertion that their method of striving after the Kingdom of God was vain. They sought to attain to such a state of complete righteousness that at last they might be vouchsafed the Kingdom of God in recompense. But Jesus saw in this conception and in such a scheme of life profound depravity (hypocrisy); it must have been impossible to him to regard righteousness as a means to an end. He accounts righteousness to be itself the content of that which makes us blessed (Matt. v. 6); it is only when they possess the Kingdom of God that men can really become righteous; for he identifies striving after righteousness with striving after the Kingdom (Matt. vi. 33). Only in the Kingdom of God can righteous persons be found. Therefore his summons to the Kingdom of God is directed not to "the righteous" but to sinners. In his proclamation of the nearness of the Kingdom of God he never suggests that the necessary amount of righteousness has been fulfilled; he says rather, Change your way of thinking! (Mark i. 15).

Secondly, Jesus differed from Jewish piety in his understanding of the other-worldly nature of the Kingdom of God. According to the Messianic hope the Kingdom of God was, it is true, to come from the other world; but that which was regarded as the content of the Kingdom of God was of this world; for it was the product of the earthly desires of men. Jesus, on the other hand, saw in the Kingdom of God no mere heightening of the natural life, and in blessedness not simply a fulfilment of the joys of the natural life; in his thought, rather, the possession of the Kingdom of God involves that a man should be free from this familiar longing of his own heart. The man who is still subject to this longing cannot, according to the thought of Jesus, really desire the rule of God (Matt. vi. 19–24). Those who have not attained to inward freedom are therefore shut out from the Kingdom of God; it would hence seem impossible for those possessed of earthly riches to enter (Mark x. 20–24). For the same reason Jesus repudiated any confusion of the Kingdom of God with political hopes (Matt. iv. 10; Mark xii. 17). Finally in his sayings about self-denial Jesus showed that the highest life which may be ours in God lies beyond the horizon of the world of natural desire.

Thus Jesus rejected all attempts to picture to ourselves the Kingdom of God as a supreme good. By this he meant that we do not understand it of ourselves, but only as it is vouchsafed to us. Faced with this attitude, we must needs ask more urgently that ever what he himself understood by the Kingdom. Yet the fact is that he never described it. His parables do not give a picture of it; they have another purpose. What Jesus sought to make clear in his preaching is something quite different. He tries continually to

make clear what real righteousness is, and he tries
to stimulate men to put their trust in the goodness
of God. It is clear in these sayings of Jesus that in
all history he was the first to express the real meaning
of moral good, that it is the Will to Fellowship, issuing
in inner freedom won in and through fellowship.
Similarly, he appears to have been the first who ven-
tured to equate the requirements of such a righteousness with the command to love God. In correlating
these two requirements and at the same time differen-
tiating between them, he expresses the very essence
of religion and morality alike. But if this constitutes
the content of those sayings of Jesus which were intended to bring home to his hearers the Kingdom of
God, what he understood by that Kingdom becomes
clear. He must have meant that the beginning of
the Kingdom of God is given to men in the stirrings
of such righteousness and such trust or religion in
their hearts.

In general, it is the way of Jesus to take the
language of Old Testament religion very seriously.
Thus he takes the expression, the Kingdom of God,
in the strict sense of the term; he understands by it
the rule of God which man may see and experience—
above all, therefore, the rule of God in man's own heart.
He who does not desire this as his supreme good, but
desires something different, cannot say with any truth
that he strives after the Kingdom of God. If he
would honestly say this, he must look for the satisfaction of his craving for life in this fact alone—that
God really rules in his heart as Lord. We are only in
reality submissive to the power of God when we stand

to him in a relationship of absolute trust, and in inward independence practise the good we know: when, that is to say, our conduct is authentic obedience.   When this is the case, we also realize that a blessed and eternal future thus opens before us.   That is why Jesus never describes the blessedness of the Kingdom of God; for those who in this way really pass under God's dominion, have personal but incommunicable experience of this blessedness.   While others, in spite of every attempt to depict it to them, can never grasp it (John iii. 3).   The blessedness of the Kingdom of God is only comprehensible to us when God himself has so inwardly transformed us that we are fully submissive to him.   How this happens, or how, according to the thought of Jesus, God's Kingdom comes to men, is our second question, to which we now pass.

17. *The Messianic power of Jesus over his first disciples.*

Even if anyone holds the tradition about Jesus to be untrustworthy as a whole, still he will not deny that it contains a life-like picture of the power which Jesus claimed and actually exercised over his disciples.   This picture is a convincing feature of the tradition, and our first task is to make it real to ourselves.   The Kingdom of God as conceived by Jesus can only be entered through an inward transformation, that is, through a change of mind, to which Jesus summons those to whom he proclaims the nearness of the Kingdom of God (Mark i. 15).   But Jesus knows that man cannot of himself generate in his own nature this new life or new disposition (Matt. xix. 26).   Man does not create the Kingdom of God; it comes upon him (Matt. xii. 28); and Jesus was aware that in his impact upon sinful men this act of God comes to pass. Thus he brings them the Kingdom of God. He therefore permits the disciples to pay him homage as Messiah (Matt. xvi. 16–17; xxi. 2–11). From the prophets, the servants of God, he distinguishes himself as the "Son of God" (Matt. xxi. 34–39); against the authority of Moses he sets his own (Matt. xix. 9). Even the least of his disciples he holds to be greater than the greatest prophet (Matt. xi. 11; xiii. 17). Similar things were no doubt said of the Messiah of Jewish expectations. But in these sayings Jesus attributes to himself unmistakably a power incomparably higher than was ever ascribed to the Jewish Messiah. This follows from the simple fact that in his teaching the Kingdom of God, which is to come through the Messiah and with him, has a meaning different from that which it bears in the Messianic hope of Israel. When he ascribed to himself the power of the Messiah to bring comfort to the heavy-laden (Matt. xi. 28), it follows from his conception of the Kingdom of God that he meant that he was able to give the people the rule of God in their souls. But that the Messiah should have this power over the soul was to the Jew of that day an unheard-of assertion; and to us, too, it remains inconceivable how a man could make such a claim for himself. According to the tradition, however, Jesus makes such a claim on other occasions too in explicit terms; he says he alone can help men really to know the Father; he can make God so real to them as to enable them to adopt towards God the attitude of a child to a father (Matt. xi. 27).

But, above all, the claim is clearly implied in the fact
that Jesus could say to those who were shaken to the
depths of their being by the impression his personality
made upon them, that their sins were pardoned. He
could not speak in this way if he were not convinced
that the impact of his personality upon them, and their
responsive trust in him, meant for them the experience alike of the judgment and of the mercy of God.
But this was in effect to proclaim that through the
power of his Person the rule of God was realized
in sinful men. Hence we read that Jesus claimed for
his Person the same unlimited devotion which is due
to God himself (Matt. x. 37–39; xvi. 25). If Jesus
could say that he who loves father or mother more
than him is unworthy of him, and that whosoever
loses his life for his sake will find it again, he must
have been convinced that his power over the hearts of
men was God's power experienced by them. In this
tradition the first disciples have put on record the
way in which he sought to affect them. And the
whole New Testament is evidence that they were certain that they had experienced this wonderful power
of Jesus over them. Let us now try to determine how
the same experience may come to us.

18. *The power of the personality of Jesus over us.*

Our Christianity would obviously be entirely different from that of the first Christian community if we
were unable to apprehend the Person of Jesus as a fact
of our own experience and a fact instinct with the same
power that the first witnesses knew. That we should
experience this is, however, roundly declared to be

superfluous and impossible by those very Christians who lay most stress upon the fact that our Christianity must be identical with that of the first Christian community.

Of course such an experience is unnecessary for those who do not long for personal and inalienable experiences of the reality of God. The man who does not look for the assurance of real religion will no doubt be content with what others say to him about God and Christ. He will even be able to derive blessing from this; but the joy and power of Christian faith remain denied to him. These can be given him only through the Person of Jesus known as an unquestionable fact of his own experience. Many things which are told about Jesus in the New Testament are not able to produce this effect upon us; when we hear about the wonderful power of Jesus over nature, that he made the dead to live again and that he himself rose from the dead, this could not in itself give us any sense of reality. We shall be able to find a significance in all these things that are told of him, but not until we have come to know Jesus himself in his inner life.

If, however, we long for a Being to whom we may surrender ourselves, then the self-evidencing picture of Jesus' inner life drawn in the New Testament is capable of gripping us with all the power of a personally experienced reality.

The perfection of this our unattained ideal confronts us with self-evidencing power in all that reveals to us his inner life. But the very One who thus stands before us as our Judge has done everything to win for himself the complete confidence of our hearts. Consequently the Person of Jesus apprehended by us in the New Testament becomes for us the pure manifestation of that Power which alone we can call God, since it alone completely takes us captive.

Now if this one gift has come to us from our own first-hand apprehension of the New Testament portrait of Jesus, we cannot possibly conceive this portrait to be a mere creation of human fancy. We are bound to see in it reminiscences of One who inspired this picture of his Person by his effect upon the hearts of men. Although this picture of Jesus so greatly surpasses all other examples of human greatness and power that it remains in the last analysis an inscrutable mystery to us, it is yet a picture that becomes to us more convincing and intimate than any other. To imagine that in all its greatness and insight it was the idealization of a prophet's imagination becomes impossible to us.

The Person of Jesus becomes to us a real Power rooted in history, not through historical proofs, but through the experience produced in us by the picture of his spiritual life which we can find for ourselves in the pages of the New Testament. We gain here an experience that we would otherwise seek in vain, the impression of a unique Person who is able to hold us in thraldom of utter surrender; we can no longer maintain an attitude of critical detachment, as we should do were we inclined to regard the tradition as a product of human imagination. Any such inclination would really indicate a belief that the traditional picture is within the scope of our own

creative abilities—which would at once destroy all
possibility of entire surrender to the personality
depicted. Everything depends therefore on whether
we really know the picture of Jesus in the New Testament, and experience in him a Power to which, with
feelings of mingled reverence and trust, we know
ourselves completely subject. Each one of us must
have this personal realization, if he is to become
like those disciples whose experience we find expressed
in the New Testament. A man cannot come to this
through others, nor can he lead others to it (cf. the
term "Holy Spirit" in the New Testament).

19. *The conception of faith in the preaching of Jesus.*
   By "faith in God" Jesus does not mean a man's
readiness to adopt a doctrine about God; rather he
understands by it a complete self-committal to the
power and goodness of God as realized in facts
(Matt. vi. 26–30; vii. 7; xiv. 31). The "faith" of
Jesus is distinguished by the following points from
the mere willingness to adopt doctrines:
   1. Jesus regards "faith" as a source of powers
which cannot be possessed apart from it. For the
right faith in God sets one entirely free from care
and despondency (Matt. vi. 30–34; Luke xii. 28). It
should thus give us the power to triumph inwardly
over the circumstances upon which we remain out-
wardly dependent. It is not, therefore, the man who
hesitates about doctrines that Jesus calls the man of
little faith, but he who in some difficult situation loses
his trust in God, and doubts whether God is present
to hear and help him (Matt. xvii. 20; Mark ii. 5).

For Jesus the man of little faith is the man who lacks courage (Matt. viii. 26). On the other hand, even the faint beginnings of real faith should at once give us the power to accomplish things which would otherwise be quite beyond our powers (Mark x. 20 f.).

2. The readiness to agree with ideas which do not express a reality that we have personally apprehended we can only regard as an arbitrary act of that free will which we so easily exercise. Whether or not such readiness is God's work in us, is a matter not of experience, but merely of opinion. Of faith as conceived by Jesus we can assert on the strength of experience that it is at once God's gift and an act of our own obedience. For this faith is patent to us as God's gift when we consider the facts through which trust in God's power and goodness was produced in us; experience also proves it to be our own act, since all trust is of necessity a free devotion or obedience to a spiritual Power whose right to rule us we acknowledge. This obedience of faith involves always the union of real joy in God, or love to him, with that fear of him which liberates from all fear of man (Matt. x. 28).

3. If Jesus understands by faith simply submission to the self-revealing God, it follows that for him faith means sincerity; for no man can be subdued in his innermost nature who refuses to give heed to that which is really the most powerful influence in his own life.

In these three respects faith, as Jesus sees it, is something entirely different from the effort to agree with notions which are not the expression of any reality that a man has personally apprehended. Such an attempt affords us no strength; we cannot experience it as God's work upon us, and it cannot be looked upon as obedience to the truth. In such an effort, which many call faith, that which ought to be the religion of the disciples of Jesus will be—not realized, but rather thwarted or spoiled.

The Christian religion or Christian faith cannot be anything else than obedience to that Power on which, as we know through our own experience, we are in our innermost nature dependent. We Christians are convinced that this power is pre-eminently manifest to us in our experience of the impact of the Person of Jesus upon us. But a man who is conscious of this cannot remain sincere except by worshipping God in this spiritual power which he experiences. In this inner constraint the Christian perceives God revealing himself to him. Our faith in God is therefore not an arbitrary thing, nor is it an illusion created by our own desire; it is the recognition of a reality apprehended by ourselves; that is to say, it is knowledge. But we possess this knowledge of God only from our own experience and only for ourselves. We cannot receive religious knowledge by having it proved to us, nor can we thus impart it to others. It must arise in each man afresh and individually; and by virtue of it he is then born into a new life.

20. *The nature and genesis of faith according to orthodox doctrine.*

The orthodox doctrine of faith was founded by Melanchthon in the later editions of the *Loci,* and it was completed by Martin Chemnitz and later by Johann Gerhardt.

The period of Protestant orthodoxy always maintained the fundamental conception of the Reformation that man is saved by faith, and that this is done in so far as faith is *fiducia*, that is, trust in God working upon us through Christ. But the orthodox conception of the genesis of such *fiducia* contradicts this first principle; according to this *fiducia* can only arise when a man has first learnt from the Scriptures the doctrines which God seeks to reveal to him, and has given his assent to them. Thus according to the orthodox doctrine the *notitia* or knowledge of the doctrines contained in the Scriptures and the *assensus* or assent to these doctrines form the basis of the *fiducia*. If this is shaken, and if the Biblical doctrines are not held to be indisputable truth, then saving faith or trust in the grace of God in Christ are made impossible.

The *notitia* and the *assensus* are distinguished in the orthodox theology under the name of *fides generalis* from the *fiducia*, which is *fides salvifica* or *specialis*. The *fides generalis*, however, must likewise be the gift of the Holy Spirit, although the actions of this faith, the *notitia* and the *assensus*, effect no inner transformation in man. The orthodox emphasize that even the entirely godless man may assent to the doctrines of salvation; even according to their teaching man's inner transformation and redemption appear only when the "confidence" in the doctrines derived from the Scriptures, or the *fides specialis*, is combined with this *fides generalis*. The saving faith which should renew a man is thus according to this view founded on a spiritual event which leaves a man unchanged in his disposition, and which is therefore obviously to be regarded as an act of the unregenerated man. To arrive at personal certitude of faith, a man must first submit himself to the authority of the Scriptures, although he has not yet attained to any inner harmony with their content. We can only experience redemption in ourselves when we have assented to the correct doctrine of redemption.

This doctrine of the nature and genesis of faith is distinguished from the Roman doctrine only by one point: it would base faith solely on the authority of the Scriptures, whilst Catholicism combines the authority of the Church with that of the Scriptures. We need only say, further, that the nature and genesis of faith is already described by Thomas Aquinas in exactly the same manner as by Melanchthon and his successors. Thomas defines faith as *cum assensu cogitare*. Of the genesis of faith he taught: *ad fidem duo requiruntur: ut credibilia proponantur et assensus credentis ad ea quae proponuntur*. He is, then, describing exactly what the orthodox theologians call *fides generalis;* like them, too, he regards these acts as only the first steps in the process of inward transformation that takes place in a Christian. The orthodox, with Luther and with the New Testament, call this πίστις, or *fiducia*. Thomas calls it for the most part *spes*; but to describe a particularly strong faith he uses also *fiducia*. In Protestant orthodoxy, therefore, it is only the mode of expression that is different; the central idea is in both cases the same, namely, that we find the God who is ready to save us and in whom we can trust only when we have decided to assent to Scriptural doctrines about him. The requirements of faith are only made more difficult in Protestant orthodoxy by the official repudiation of the Catholic expedient of *fides implicita*.

Correct elements in this doctrine are: (1) That the first thing in faith is the *notitia*—man can only find revelation in that with which he has entered into some spiritual connection; (2) that faith can never exist without assent to the conceptions which are first introduced to a man from the Scriptures through Christian preaching; (3) that a man can only be considered a believing Christian when he has come to a heart-felt trust in God. But the doctrine of the way of attaining to this, or the doctrine of the genesis of faith, is erroneous.

1. It would be untruthful, and therefore a sin, to resolve to assent to the doctrines prescribed by the Scriptures or the Church, when one had not yet apprehended their truth. It is nonsense to maintain that a sin can be the condition for the inward renewal of the sinner through the grace of God.

2. A faith which is to make a new being of a man cannot have its origin in a spiritual act which the "unregenerate" man accomplishes. The doctrine of Paul, according to which a man cannot be redeemed through his own works, but by faith alone, becomes nonsense if faith is regarded as legal rectitude achieved by unredeemed man. Paul himself declared the fulfilling of such mere legalism to be sin (Rom. xiv. 23).

3. The judgment of faith itself as to its own genesis is very different from the judgment of orthodoxy.

For if Christians are fundamentally persuaded that what is asserted by faith, in contradiction to the senses and to the intellect, represents reality, then they will never ascribe it to their own efforts, but to the power of an experience bestowed upon them.

Without the conviction of a reality apprehensible only by faith, the *fiducia* or saving faith can never exist; but the Christian must experience the genesis of this conviction as God's work; it is included in the experience which creates pure trust in us. It is because there has been misunderstanding on this point that the Evangelical Church is brought back again in the orthodox doctrine to the fundamental conception of Roman Christianity. A redemption *sola fide* can no longer be asserted if faith itself is experienced solely as an act which unregenerate man ought and is easily able to perform.

21. *The Scriptures as the source of Christian doctrine.*

The Reformation opposed to the Roman Church the fundamental principle that Christian doctrine is to be derived from the Scriptures alone. Everything depends, therefore, on a correct definition of this principle of the authority of Scripture adopted by the Evangelical Christianity that appeared in the Reformation.

It would be un-Christian if it meant the acknowledgment of any chance sentence of the Scriptures as God's word, by which a Christian ought to be guided in his life, and the community in its doctrine. Such a principle of the authority of Scripture would set a book above God's revelation, which we can receive only through personal influences, above all from the personal life of Jesus. If a Christian has come to recognize the constraining power which comes upon him from the Person of Jesus as a revelation of God, he can take as a word of God only that which is in some way recognizable as an expression of this fact. The Evangelical principle of the authority of Scripture can therefore, rightly understood, only mean this: that what we should apprehend in the Scriptures as the indispensable means to Salvation is what God is seeking to say to us through the personal life revealing itself there, and pre-eminently through the power of the Person of Jesus. Everything else in the Scriptures can have for us the value of a word of God only as we understand it either as an introduction to what we find in Jesus, or as an effect of his power. Next to the Person of Jesus, what we must look for in Scripture is the personal experience of men who long for redemption, and the personal experience of his disciples whose life is radiant with the consciousness of redemption. It is these three facts that we should try to understand as God's word directed towards us. That which we are unable to connect in some way with these manifestations of personal life is not yet for us a word of God. At any moment of our inner development, therefore, we can point to some parts of the Scriptures which do not have for us the significance of the word of God. But this does not rule out the possibility that these very parts of the Scriptures may have possessed that significance for other people or may still possess it, or that they may one day possess it for us as well.

## 22. *The foundation of the Evangelical principle of the authority of Scripture.*

The man whom Christ has lifted up to God sees in the Biblical tradition through which this Redeemer is given to him the work of his God. If he has in consequence attained to the religious standpoint of faith, or to the attitude of entire surrender to the spiritual Power there revealed, then he can regard historical investigations of the Bible with equanimity. He will take advantage of any help he can derive from them towards the clearer apprehension of the one thing that he seeks in it, the faith of the Bible and the Bible's God. Criticism may discover much which renders Scriptural statements doubtful; yet the Christian, if the Bible has once united him to the God who redeems him, will nevertheless be persuaded that he receives through the Bible everything that he needs for the life that is life indeed. The Scriptures are in this respect absolutely perfect. Our faith in the Bible springs from our personal experience in regard to it. Such a confidence in it can arise only from the fact that we have found in it him whose creative power we experience in ourselves, the God who reveals himself in its faith and its Christ. Schleiermacher (*Glaubenslehre,* §128) and Kahler (*Das Offenbarungs-ansehen der Bibel,* 1903) are therefore right when they say: We do not believe in Christ because of the Bible, but we believe in the Bible because we have found Christ in it.

The case would be entirely different did not the Bible itself provide Christians with the means to prove that the Scriptures are unassailable as regards this the most important part of their contents. If apart from such a position in regard to the Scriptures, one still maintains that they deserve unqualified confidence, there is no way open save that taken by Judaism at the time of Jesus.

That is to say, one must suppose that through the manner of their origin the Scriptures are guaranteed against any error. This supposition that the books of the Bible came into existence as the work of the Spirit of God, free from error in every particular, is found, for instance, in Philo, but it was also worked out elsewhere in the greatest detail by the Jewish theology of that age. From Judaism it passed over into the Roman Church; finally it became a refuge for the Churches of the Reformation, when they could no longer follow Luther in finding the indubitable and marvellous revelation in a particular aspect of the Bible's content. This doctrine of "inspiration" has now become so untenable in Evangelical Christianity that it no longer finds any theological support.

We must, however, emphasize the fact that in Protestantism this doctrine has been elaborated in two ways which distinguish it from the Jewish and Roman doctrine: (1) orthodox Protestantism teaches that the Holy Scriptures possess an *auctoritas causativa;* that is, the Bible produces the acknowledgment of its own truth by the power of the spirit inherent in it; (2) like Luther orthodox Protestantism rejects allegorical exegesis, and demands that the interpretation of the Scripture texts should be bound by that plain meaning of the words which we can ourselves determine. But in so doing the Protestant doctrine admitted the right of historical criticism, which inevitably disposes of the doctrine itself. For the orthodox presupposition about the Bible is rendered untenable by the variant readings established by textual criticism.

### 23. *The scientific task of systematic theology.*

Christian faith is that renewal of the inner life which men experience in contact with Jesus as he becomes for them that revelation of God which is the foundation of God's rule in their hearts. It is an inward bond between Christians that this fact they have themselves experienced has become the most powerful factor in their lives. The Christian community which thus comes into existence has its unity in the fact that the life-story of all its members is fundamentally the same, and that each of them accordingly desires to contemplate in the others this spiritual possession. They have attained to the moral seriousness required to reflect upon the import of their experiences and to ask which is the most significant of them all; and they have then found their answer in their contact with the Person of Jesus. Such an origin lays upon the Christian community a scientific task which was first rightly grasped by Schleiermacher (*Der Christliche Glaube nach den Grundsätzen der evangelischen Kirche,* 1821 and 1830).

The task is this: With a view to the preservation of their community Christians must bring to consciousness the way in which the new kind of life arises, and the way in which it expresses itself. The proper expression of Christian faith is the man who has been brought to "newness of life" through it. He is therefore at all times the indispensable means for the propagation of the Christian faith amongst mankind. But the forms of this new life are thoughts and motives which can only be true and effective for this purpose in the case of a man whom God has set free. Evangelical theology is obliged by its estimate of the Scriptures to find there the classical expression of this spiritual life. The means of understanding this content of the Scripture is, apart from historical investigation, the personal faith of the theologian. On the other hand, this faith is not the source from which theology may obtain the view of the new life set free by God. Schleiermacher did not entirely escape the danger of falling into this mistake, and the danger is still more apparent in some of his followers (Hofmann, Frank). Evangelical dogmatic has rather to obtain from the Scriptures the knowledge of the reality hidden from the natural man and unveiled to the eye of faith.

Before Schleiermacher a very different task was essayed by systematic theology, the most important representatives of which were Thomas Aquinas (*Summa totius theologiæ*) and Calvin (*Institutio religionis christianæ*). The old theology did not set out to understand a new life created through God's revelation, to understand it in its origin and the interworking of its powers; it sought to compile doctrines purporting to set before us God's revelation in the form of a code vouchsafed by God. It then sought to demonstrate the rationality of some part at least of these doctrines. Out of these proofs of the old theology has developed rationalism, which severs Christianity from its historical roots and then threatens it with ruin. For doctrines whose ideas were not conceived as the forms of a new life could be proved only by conceiving them as rational and thus misunderstanding them. Hence, in Protestantism at least there arose a desire to prove the truth of as much as possible of Christian doctrine, and a tendency to throw over all those doctrines for which such proof was unobtainable. This tendency culminated in the Rationalism of the eighteenth century.

Schleiermacher not only fought against the rationalistic conception of religion; he was the first to recognize that the subject of theology cannot be doctrines or dogmas, but an inner quickening created in mankind through the power of the Person of Jesus. He showed that the new task of theology must be to depict this new life in its uniqueness and wonder. This marked the victory over Rationalism. The idea that doctrine must be rational was superseded as soon as it was recognized that in fact Christian doctrine is only to be understood as the expression of new personal life. For that which is living, always, by its very nature, transcends the merely rational. At the same time, that which in the older theology had led to rationalism was thereby put out of court for all those who had grasped this new point of view. For he who is conscious of the way in which, through full surrender, a new life grows up within him, knows why the ideas involved in this new life are true, and knows why for others they must seem false.

24. *The systematic treatment of the ideas involved in
faith.*

In the new life created in us by the power of Jesus
we obtain the strength to overcome the world and sin.
In this way we become aware of the importance of
the historical forces through which this is mediated
to us.   The first section in Part II will show how we
overcome the world in the consciousness of God's
working through Christ; the second section, how we
overcome sin; the third section, how in consequence
we conceive of the historical facts by which we are
thus transformed: (1) the Person of Jesus; (2) the
Spirit working in the community.   At the end of the
course the knowledge of the nature of God which is
implied in this divine activity will be summed up in the
Christian doctrine of the Trinity.

*PART II*

# THE FAITH OF EVANGELICAL
# CHRISTIANITY

# THE OVERCOMING OF THE WORLD BY THE FAITH CREATED BY GOD

## CHAPTER V

## THE KNOWLEDGE OF GOD THROUGH FAITH

*25. The task of systematic theology prescribed by Christian faith.*

Our religion is God's work in us. The Biblical name for this religion is faith. The faith intended by Scripture is therefore not the arbitrary acceptance of ideas, but it is that submission to God to which we are brought by the power of God that we have ourselves experienced. But if God rules in us, our surrender to him sets us free from all that is hostile to our true life. Consequently faith, in the Scriptural sense, itself constitutes the true life of the redeemed man. This knowledge, to which expression is given in the loftiest reaches of Biblical piety, was rediscovered in the Reformation, but Schleiermacher was the first to perceive that this discovery involved of necessity a new kind of systematic theology.

Catholic Christianity is fundamentally unscriptural;

for to it faith means the acceptance of ideas with
which, personally, a man may or may not be able to
agree. The Catholic Christian is told by the Church
which doctrines are divine revelations and therefore
demand obedience. By the act of assent to these
doctrines a man may earn blessedness. It follows
that we have a right to demand of Catholic theology
(1) that it should exactly formulate these doctrines,
and (2) that it should show that their acceptance is
possible for a reasonable man. The classical model of
this undertaking is still the *Summa totius theologiæ* of
Thomas Aquinas. In the main he has been closely
followed by the theologians of the Reformation
Churches in the first three centuries. The best work
of this kind is to this day Calvin's *Institutio religionis
christianæ*, 1559. Schleiermacher was the first to
perceive that the understanding of faith or of religion
regained in the Reformation demanded not only a
change of particular doctrines, but a theology different
in kind from that of the scholastics. He rejected
the attempt to formulate doctrines through the
acceptance of which a man would become a believer.
On the contrary, he sought to conceive and describe
the Christian faith as itself a life issuing from God.
This Christian faith is, to be sure, the same religion
which one may also mark at an earlier date in
the purest forms of Old Testament piety. But in
the case of Christians, the consciousness of being
redeemed by God is always bound up with remem-
brance of Jesus Christ. To come to know this One
is for them the experience that eclipses every other
cause of thankfulness to God. A systematic theology

which aims at making explicit for the Christian what is given him in his faith has then two tasks. It has to show (1) how a man is inwardly renewed through the experience he may have of the power of the Person of Jesus, (2) how the faith—grounded in this experience and determined by it as to content—expresses itself.

This second problem we shall deal with later on in Section II of this part, when we shall expound the ideas which are the expression of the faith which knows itself sustained by the power of the personal life of Jesus. Following this path, however, we shall never obtain a closed and entirely consistent system of ideas; for faith itself grows, it changes daily, if it is really alive (Rom. xii. 2), and is continually producing ideas which are in a state of mutual tension.

## 26. *The unity of God.*

The inward transaction which Scripture calls faith is in itself the only possible knowledge of God. If we experience anything which brings us to pure devotion, it is always the beginning of real knowledge of God, and at the same time a beginning of true faith. Faith produced by such an experience need not, then, go on to ask how it can make a knowledge of God its own; for it already possesses it implicitly. Rather will it be its highest duty to grasp and to hold fast with the utmost conscientiousness that which it has so received. This will be possible for us only if we seek in the Scriptures for the richest manifestation of a personal life that is ruled by God. There only do we get a perfect picture of what can be made of a man by God's rule in his soul.

This value of the Scriptures, constantly re-experienced in the Christian community, finds expression in the Reformers' "principle of the authority of Scripture." In order to preserve the Christian community from gross errors, the public preaching of the Gospel should be closely related to Scripture conceptions. But the requirements of this principle can only be satisfied on two conditions: first, we must be in a position to search out in the Scriptures those ideas which impress us as belonging to faith; second, obedience to Scripture should be required of no man as regards those passages in which he personally does not hear God speak to him. Otherwise one is making faith a thing external to our own natures, a thing which contradicts the will of God. We all know parts of Scripture which are such that they induce nothing of that experience of the power of God which bows our soul in willing surrender. The birth of faith within ourselves is the sole means whereby we may distinguish between such passages of Scripture and those others in which we can apprehend God for ourselves. Scripture, therefore, as Hofmann and Frank on the Lutheran side have particularly emphasized, can be received as the word of God only by the community of the faithful.

If, then, faith has arisen in us out of serious reflection on our own intuitions, we can understand at once why monotheism is the fundamental idea both of the Old Testament and of the New; for our faith arises from the realization that we are subject to a spiritual Power that is actually in touch with us. But in the consciousness that it so works upon us we clearly recognize this Power as something which cannot co-exist with anything else of its kind. That is also the significance of the Biblical conception that there is but one God (Mark xii. 29–30; Matt. vi. 24). The problem of the nature of God does not find its solution in a doctrine of one uniform ground of the universe, but in our actually becoming conscious of the one and only Power to whom we ourselves can utterly submit. Jesus consummated the monotheism of the Old Testament not only through the discovery of this connection, but also through the power of his Person, through which he becomes for us the one satisfying Way of Knowledge, in presence of which there is nothing left for us but utter surrender in reverence and trust. But if the conception of the unity of God has thus become vital to our own faith, then this conception is immediately connected with that of God as transcendent or invisible. For a Being who is unique in kind cannot belong to the reality cognizable by science or by the world.

### 27. *God as our Father.*

As disciples of Jesus we should call upon God always as our Father. Everything in which a man may experience God at work in the creation of faith was for Jesus summed up in this word: Father. But at the same time he reminds us of what hinders in us men the power that inwardly constrains or wins the heart of a child.

Jesus refers to the fact that the human father is selfish (Matt. vii. 11). Through injury which the child inflicts upon him the kindness in him may be destroyed.

He lacks, too, the power to help the child in all its necessities. It is not so with God. He is not embittered through man's trespass (Matt. v. 45; Luke xv.), and he always answers the requests that are really directed to him (Matt. vii. 7 f.). His care operates in the smallest details of our existence (Matt. x. 30), that is to say, in the whole reality in which we live. In a word, it means that God's goodness in the redemption of man is inexhaustible. It follows that the one thing that can make us blessed is his rule in our hearts (Matt. vi. 33). From him alone can we expect that which is truly good.

Again, there must always be combined with devotion to him the corresponding aversion from all that is contradictory to his nature. He who loves God with heartfelt trust can never hate that which is living. But he should always hate the powers that obstruct life. He who fulfils neither of these conditions puts himself thereby outside the sphere of God's goodness; for a goodness which would affirm its own contradiction would annul itself. Pure goodness therefore cannot further a state of mind in opposition to its essential character. It embraces only natures which will let it make them alive or free. But then God's goodness is in itself righteousness, just as also his righteousness is goodness (1 John i. 9). Only when we set God's goodness before us as our goal can we feel ourselves to be children of God (Matt. v. 44 f.). Only a being in whom there exists the will to be the instrument of his goodness can be an object of his goodness. But since we never attain to that entirely, the man who can really trust in God will at the same time fear him more than aught else (Matt. x. 28). Therefore with the love of God there is always combined in struggling men its opposite, the fear of God.

The sayings of Jesus, then, lead faith to the knowledge that in experiencing the reality of God we perceive in him at the same time the basis of our confidence and our moral end. God is, then, the Creator of our inner life or of our real self. That is what Jesus meant when he called God our Father.

As devotion to the God who works upon us issues in the knowledge that he is the sole ground of our true life, our monotheism is deepened. We then begin to see something which the reason cannot grasp, a conception which Israel never quite reached, that justice and loving-kindness are one. But at the same time we have to face the fact that with us men devotion to God is in constant danger of perversion into the fear that flees from before him.

## 28. *God as the Father of Jesus Christ.*

Christian faith means the assurance that in all our experiences there works upon us, even though hidden from us, a goodness as inexhaustible as reality itself. But the recollection of experiences which once produced such an assurance in us may be so thrown into the background by our present plight that we now feel ourselves abandoned by God. In this situation Christian faith experiences a succor which men of other faiths lack. The Christian may find himself in such case, but he is able inwardly to overcome it; for the Christian community finds in the New Testament a foundation for its faith unknown to such as are either ignorant of this traditon or heedless of it. To be sure, not even the Christian can derive the foundation of an indestructible assurance simply from the New Testament conception of God's fatherly goodness. Whoever attempts to do so will soon see why such a thought cannot produce in the man who in his despair seeks after God the faith that overcomes his difficulties. Only the actual creation of faith in his own heart can open a man's eyes to God's goodness as the power that saves him. This can be brought about neither by the joy of a happy lot nor by what we learn from others of the goodness of God. The assurance that in all our experiences God's sheer goodness surrounds us is thus for the religious man simply the expression of his faith; it can never appear to him the ground of his faith. Faith can find its basis only in the experience which produced it. This is always a happening in which a man becomes aware of the spiritual Power to which alone he can surrender himself without compunction. But we Christians are the only people who find this occurrence in a fact which cannot be obscured for us by any new experiences, since we have only to think of it to see it standing before us again as something indestructible and incomparably great.

For our most important experience, which is the real basis of our inner life, is for us the fact that we have met with the Person of Jesus as manifested in the New Testament. We are Christians in virtue of our consciousness of the power of the Person of Jesus over us. We have this experience, however, only when we take to heart as a unique, incomparable gift the following characteristics of the portrait of Jesus.

The picture which the Evangelists have given us of the life of Jesus is that of a battle against evil and of a life of service to those who despair of themselves. Besides this we find sayings which bring home to us with an unfathomable simplicity the only life in which we can truly live, the good which we ought to do, and the God in whom we should trust. Historical criticism may and even must question the certitude of this tradition; but we ourselves see as a fact that in all that is there given us to enable us to make clear to ourselves the inner life of Jesus, there is no trait to be found which could cast a shadow on the picture of his goodness and of his strong earnestness. The content of this picture will therefore convince everyone with eyes to see it that it is not a man-made fiction, but the expression of a wonderful historical reality. Thus Jesus becomes for us the evidence of the reality of the God whom he calls his Father; for every feature of the tradition in which we find his inner life expressed combines to depict a man who derives from his confidence in God the power to accomplish the greatest tasks and to bear the heaviest burdens. Thus once our eyes are open to see him, while we can indeed think of ourselves without God, we can never so think of him.

## 29. *God as the Lord of the World.*

The Power to which we know ourselves to be subjected in free surrender is already in fact conceived by us as that which rules the universe; for we could not surrender ourselves utterly to a Being whom we did not regard in this light. The very experience, then, which brings us to the point of worshipping with perfect trust the Power which touches us in that experience, or of calling that Power God, produces in us the idea of omnipotence.

That God is almighty means, in the first place, that there are no external limits set to his activity (Luke i. 37; Matt. xix. 26). This thought, however, has its necessary complement in a second one, that everything that is, even the most hidden motions of our own souls, is the work of God. Luther, therefore, in his writing *De servo arbitrio,* 1525, accounted the refusal of Erasmus to acknowledge this conclusion as denoting an entire lack of faith and of real religion. Though he did Erasmus wrong in this, it yet remains true that our faith is impeded so long as we fail to recognize in everything that may befall us the evidence of God's care for us. Inasmuch as Jesus acknowledges this specific providence of God in his own case, and commends to his disciples the same attitude, he really employs the completely developed idea of omnipotence without expressly formulating it. On the other hand, express reference is made to God's all-working power in Rom. viii. 28 and Acts xvii. 28.

It is obvious, however, that this unqualified idea of the omnipotence of God is not at all times the expression of our experience at the moment; it expresses our experience only when faith has overcome some hindrance against which it had to do battle. In the actual struggle of faith, on the other hand, we cannot get beyond the expression of the idea

of omnipotence that we find in the saying of Jesus
in Matt. xix. 26, that God can do everything that
he wills to do. Yet we really trust in God's
omnipotence whenever the consciousness of his nearness gives us the strength to accept that which must
be (cf. Mark xiv. 36), even when we cannot understand
its necessity and when we are filled with the hopes of
a future rich beyond our understanding (Eph. iii. 20).
The working of God's omnipotence remains, nevertheless, hidden from us; it can never be sensibly perceptible in the world. For it is always in a quiet
rule over all existence that it is exercised, never in a
battle with other powers; and it is only in such a
struggle that it could be sensibly perceived. The
thought thus becomes full-fledged in our minds that
God is always hidden and his ways and judgments are
inscrutable.[1]

---

[1] Two years earlier this paragraph continued as follows:—

" This conception, necessary to religion, of God's omnipotent and therefore hidden working cannot be reconciled with the only view of personal life possible to us; for we know the latter only as a life that
realizes itself in struggle; thus everything that our knowledge pred-
icates of personal life must always contain an element inapplicable to
God Almighty. God is therefore hidden not only in his almighty working, but also in the manner of his personal life. A spiritual Being
for whom, in everything that exists or happens, there is always an
antecedent element of personal knowledge and will, is to us inconceivable.
The notion of orthodox theology that God remains hidden even from
the eye of faith to which he has revealed himself, is therefore thoroughly
justified, though the arguments adduced are inadequate.

" From the impossibility of applying to God our view of personal
life, Pantheism takes occasion to deduce that we may make absolutely
no assertion about the Personality of God (D. F. Strauss). But, on the
contrary, the idea of personality is the correct category to apply to
him to whom alone we may ascribe the power over all; for only a personal
Being has power over himself and therefore power over others who

*Footnote continued on next page*

have come to the point of facing for themselves the task of personal life. Similarly, we can think of the realization of the ideal of personal life only in Almighty God; for absolute independence, which remains for us an unattained ideal, can be real only in a Being who does not need to be continually determined by another power outside himself; that is to say, it can be real only in the Power which is over all. We recognize that our conception of personal life does not apply to God; this and the necessarily hidden manner of his working constitutes the limit of our knowledge of God; but the idea of personality is not in itself incompatible with the thought of an Almighty God."

## CHAPTER VI

# THE WORKING OF THE TRANSCENDENT GOD IN THE WORLD, AS REVEALED TO FAITH (GOD'S WORLD)

30. *The Universe.*[1]

To faith the world is a different thing from what it is to the man who does not know God. When faith rises in us we see a world completely transformed (2 Cor. v. 17); for the God who reveals himself to us thereby unifies the world for us. Previously it was to us a plurality totally unintelligible in its limitless extent. On the other hand, so far as we know ourselves laid hold upon by God, a change takes place in us whereby the world becomes for us the expression of his working. Hence all events have for faith a certain unity in so far as in all of them the believer recognizes as the motive power the love of God directed towards himself.

This spiritual victory over the world through really perfected inward devotion to God is expressed in the first sentence of Scripture. The world maintains even for this Scriptural faith its mysterious infinity. But as the creation of his God it ceases to be for the

---

[1] Thus in 1913. In 1915 the title ran : The working of the transcendent God in the creation of the Universe.

believer an occasion of anxiety. The Biblical conception, then, of the creation of the world by God does
not mean an attempt to explain the world by its
causes; it is rather a repudiation of all such efforts.
In this respect the thinking of faith knew from the
beginning that to which science has attained but
slowly in the course of the last few centuries. But in
their positive conception of the world faith and
scientific thinking remain fundamentally different;
for science as such naturally knows no totality of the
world, but only an endless "becoming" in time and
space. On the other hand, the following considerations explain how the trust in God which is his work
in us leads to the conception of an essentially limited
universe:

First: Our faith distinguishes between the world
extending in endless time and the eternal God. In
the language of sensuous perception Scripture expresses
this distinction between God and the world when it
says that God is in heaven—a heaven from which,
however, Old Testament religion had already learned
to dissociate a spatial definition (1 Kings viii. 27).

Secondly: From the standpoint of our faith this
world, as distinguished from God, is entirely dependent
on him. Its existence is founded simply upon the
motion of his Spirit, which accomplishes its task by
the Word (Heb. xi. 3).

Thirdly: The Christian sees in the world the instrument of God's revelation. (Rom. i. 20). He knows
himself to be everywhere surrounded by God, and is
convinced that nothing in the world can avail to separate him from God (Rom. viii. 39).

Fourthly: The Christian sees in the world the means to an end which God for his own sake eternally wills, or through which he is blessed (1 Cor. viii. 6; Col. i. 16). It is only in the capacity, not yet reached in the Old Testament, to conceive of the boundless world as a means to an end intelligible to men, yet beyond this world, that the idea of a universe finds a firm basis in thought.

The justification of this idea cannot, however, be based upon scientific proof. These conceptions of faith are produced ever anew through a working of God upon us which creates faith in us. Therefore they always stand opposed to that which remains unintelligible and terrifying to us in actual events. Faith, then, does not present us with a philosophy that solves the riddle of the world, but its own origin contains the promise that it will receive power to overcome the world.

## 31. *The miracle of faith.*

Any event in which we clearly perceive the impinging of God upon our own life we call a miracle. Faith sees miracle, therefore, pre-eminently in the answers God gives to its prayers. But even when the events remain unintelligible to a believer he is confident that God in his secret working through the world of the infinite accomplishes that which his child needs. Faith knows itself to be surrounded by miracles even where it perceives none.

The assertion of the old dogmatics, that a miracle is *supra et contra naturam,* is correct. For a miracle originates from a transcendent reality; it is therefore to be defined only in contrast with nature, though it is within the sphere of nature that it is experienced. The attempt to make miracle intelligible inevitably annuls the idea of miracle. We must frankly concede the logical contradiction which is involved in it. The contradiction is seen in the following consideration:

An event that takes place in the natural order we can conceive only as issuing from the causal nexus of nature. This naturally applies also to the event which we call a miracle. Hence here also we are bound to see a regular event resulting from earlier happenings. At the same time, however, we maintain that it is a new creative act of God accomplished for our sake, or that it has its origin with reference to our present need.

Against the reproach of others that this is logically impossible, faith cannot defend itself. Those religious people who, none the less, attempt a defence show in so doing that they are secretly ashamed of their faith before men. In spite of this contradiction faith firmly maintains that God performs such miracles for the faithful; for it can justify this conception to itself. The believer can conceive it true, because he recognizes in God the transcendent Lord over all, whose care is over every moment of our lives. If we trust firmly to our experience of the power of God, this already involves the thought that God at every moment is making the universe, in all its seeming infinitude, a means of succoring our life. But how God could move the universe on our behalf is a question which we certainly cannot answer; for to us the universe is an endless nexus bound by law. Naturally, too,

we are unable to refute others who are bound
to explain away miracle as impossible for the very
reason that they lack the simple experience from
which, through reflection on the most significant
moments of our life, we derive our conception of
miracle.

But we must abandon the assertion of the old
dogmatics that in the miracles which he does for us
God breaks through the natural order; for this is
the expression not of a conception of faith, but of the
attempt, antithetic to faith, to explain God's miracle.
Such an idea would, moreover, as Spinoza correctly
observed in his *Tractatus theologico-politicus*, gainsay
faith's conception of God's omnipotence.

32. *The attitude of faith to the miracles related in
      Scripture.*

Our faith can only recognize miracle when in an
event within our own experience we recognize the
impact upon our life of a power not ourselves. Hence
comes our attitude to the Biblical miracles. He
who asks himself whether he finds in the Scriptures
unquestionable facts which he experiences as God's
working upon him will scarcely be able to give an
affirmative answer. From this it follows that for
every Christian the importance of these miraculous
events of tradition must be entirely overshadowed by
that which in his own life impresses him as a miracle
of God. The word of God which we apprehend as
addressed to us personally must be more important
to us than anything else. He who refuses to admit
this refuses obedience to God.

But, for all that, every Christian will in the end declare that contact with the faith expressed in Scripture has been to him the clearest manifestation of God.  If it is so with us, then the miraculous events related in Scripture may become realities which we should not like to dispense with.  This is the normal experience of most Christians.  But if this position is not to be fraught with dangers we must in the first place keep clearly in mind the fact that such a satisfaction with the stories of miracle, a satisfaction that has come into being in us in such a way, is not faith itself, but only a concomitant of faith.  In the second place, for many Christians the scientific knowledge which they have had to acquire in the exercise of their calling has to-day made this concomitant of faith impossible in their case.  Whoever lays it down that no faith at all is possible unless a man makes up his mind to uphold the veracity of these narratives, by such insistence destroys in himself the elements of faith.  In the third place we must let ourselves be guided by the information given us in the oldest tradition as to Jesus' own attitude to his miracles. According to this tradition as a whole, Jesus exercised over nature a power unknown to us.  According to Matt. xi. 4–6 he saw in the fact that such a power was given to him a sign of his divine calling.  But he cared little for the excitement of the masses who experienced or witnessed his miraculous healings. He even tried to prevent popular ferment, in so far as he constantly bade the witnesses of his miracles to keep silence about them.  He withdrew from the populace who sought him as a miracle-monger.  The

people who would follow him for such reasons he
sternly repelled. To an extremely credulous man of
this kind such as Herod he vouchsafed, according to
Luke xxiii. 9, not a word. Finally, we never hear
that he made the willing acceptance of miraculous
stories a condition of discipleship. On the contrary
he required of his disciples something quite different,
something which no man can bestow upon himself,
namely, that they should themselves experience and
perform miracles (Matt. xvii. 20; xix. 26; xxi. 21).
This could happen in their case in virtue of faith, not
faith which they produced in themselves, but faith
given them by God as the beginning of a new life
(cf. the parable of the grain of mustard-seed). From
all this it follows that Jesus did not regard his power
over nature as the proper object of faith. To him
such miracles had quite a different significance. He
used them as means to direct to his own person
people who had witnessed such things, so that in
contact with him they might experience God's power
for themselves. He did not see the miracle that
saves men in that which was sensibly perceptible—
that is to say, in that which the godless could see
as well; but the saving miracle lay in the way in
which the impact of his Person conquered men's
hearts.

It belongs to polytheistic piety to suppose that
God's working reveals itself to men in extraordinary
events which can be verified as occurring in space.
When, on the other hand, the idea of the complete
omnipotence of God comes to full recognition—when,
that is to say, we arrive at monotheistic piety—the

earlier conception must be laid aside. We thus see how the life of Jesus is the supreme instance of the banishing of the polytheistic outlook. In spite of his conscious power over nature he did not see in such sensibly perceptible activity the miracle through which God's working was experienced; the miracle lay in his Person, whose power every man may experience for himself, though he cannot impart his experience to others. On the other hand, both polytheistic piety and the Catholic Church alike explicitly maintain the view that God's miracles are to be established as appearing in space or as sensibly perceptible. They have not yet realized that the working of Omnipotence necessarily remains beyond the reach of sensible perception.

# CHAPTER VII

# THE MAN OF GOD

### 33. *God's image in man.*

In Genesis (i. 26–27) it is simply related that God created man in his image; in the New Testament, however, this thought is an expression of faith in God, and at the same time it is precisely laid down how man may have fellowship with the Divine Being. For to say that God wishes to be our Father would be empty words unless it meant that God finds his own blessedness in making us blessed in fellowship with him. But fellowship with us can be blessedness for God only if he sees growing up in us a life which like his own is exalted above that seeming life which is of the world. Only as we are willing to rise above that seeming life can we belong to God. Our confidence that we are akin to him is therefore always at the same time a consciousness that a transcendent life has begun in us. This is most simply expressed when it is said that Jesus' disciples should feel themselves to be God's children. We can conceive of such an experience as possible only in the case of men, not in the case of other living beings known to us, since we do not perceive in the life of the latter any tendency to rise above the world.

The idea that man possesses a life akin to the divine is not derived from such a source by the piety of the Old Testament. This difference between the Old Testament and the New is linked with another. In Genesis the image of God is clearly understood as shown in the powers which man received at the Creation. This idea persists in pre-Christian religion. On the other hand, the saying of Jesus in Matt. v. 45 shows that, in his view, what connects man with God is not a power inherent in man's nature, but a task which is set him. According to that saying man is to become God's child by the exercise of that pure charity which identifies itself with its object, and is thus creative life. In the view of the Old Testament man's true nature was realized at the beginning of history; in the New Testament it appears in the course of history. To the disciples of Jesus man created after the likeness of God means a kind of life which must first be attained. They must put off the old man and put on the new man which has been created after God (Eph. iv. 24; 1 Cor. xv. 45). Here the advantage of man over all other creatures does not mean an actual possession bound up with his life, part of the endowment belonging to his position within nature. Man is rather called to become himself a being with a real life of his own, of a kind that can have no earthly origin. That which makes man such a being or an image of God is in itself inexhaustible (Rom. xiii. 8; 1 Cor. xiii. 8), while everything that belongs to earth comes to an end. It is due to this fact that man's death is judged differently in the New Testament and in the eyes of the world.

The anthropological ideas which are to be found elsewhere in the Bible can play no part in Protestant dogmatics; for we are at a loss to see how their appearance in us should be the outcome of the faith created in us by the power of the Person of Jesus.

34. *Christian faith and the freedom of the human will.*

Since faith produces in us the New Testament conception of man's essential nature, two thoughts confront each other in our consciousness in a contradiction which we cannot completely resolve.

First, faith sees itself to be the new and real life which is the creation of an almighty love. The basis of its life is thus God's action in it. This finds expression in the idea of a regeneration or in that of a new creation (John iii. 3; 2 Cor. v. 17; Gal. vi. 15). We have, then, to thank not ourselves, but God for what this faith makes of us (1 Cor. iv. 7; xv. 10). Our destiny depends on God's purpose (Rom. viii. 28–30). What brings us to salvation is not our own efforts, but God's mercy (Rom. ix. 16). Yes, and what is more, our very will is of God's working (Phil. ii. 13). Thus our real life is found only in unqualified dependence on God's omnipotence.

At this point, however, arises the second element in faith, which cannot be logically combined with the first. We cannot regard our dependence as unqualified unless it is such as is willed by ourselves. For if there remains any inward resistance our dependence is obviously not complete. If, then, we can possess real life only in free dependence upon God, we see that the origin of this life lies unquestionably in our

own free act. Necessarily, therefore, the consciousness
of our free will arises in faith not from a logical deduc-
tion, but from actual surrender to God's universal
life-creating activity. Both ideas are combined in the
New Testament in the thought that God has given us
to have life in ourselves (John v. 26). The Apostle
therefore sees in faith not only God's gift, as in
Eph. ii. 8, but also an act of human obedience, as in
Rom. i. 5; xvi. 26. We should work out our own
salvation, although we do not fail to recognize that
it is God who produces in us the willing and the
working (Phil. ii. 12 f.). Paul says, indeed (Rom. ix.
16), that our salvation does not depend on our willing
and striving; nevertheless, he summons us in 1 Cor. ix.
24 to strive after salvation. As in the preaching of
Jesus himself so throughout the whole of the New
Testament we find both conceptions combined, that of
the creation of real life by God and that of the rise
of this life by man's free act. Regeneration and conversion are, therefore, two logically opposed yet equally
necessary thoughts in regard to the origin of real life
within us.

There was consequently no justification for Luther's
unwillingness to apply to man the idea of the freedom
of the will and his claiming it for God alone. *Liberum
arbitrium est prorsus divinum nomen.* A different
judgment is expressed in the New Testament
(Matt. xxiii. 37; John v. 26), and Luther himself
employs the idea of human liberty as soon as he deals
with the ever new task of conversion. But Luther
was entirely right in declaring the contradiction
between the thought of God's omnipotence and that

of the freedom of the human will to be insoluble (*pugnat ex diametro Dei omnipotentia cum nostro libero arbitrio*).   In spite of this contradiction faith gives rise to both thoughts; in religion every moment of life involves a subduing of that which threatens to destroy in us the assurance of new life.   Yet our own act is felt by us as the coming to fruition of that which creates trust within us.   The thoughts of God's omnipotence and of our free will which arise from this do not find their justification in their consistency with one another and with other thoughts, but in the fact that they owe their origin to faith as the expression of definite moments of its life.

## 35. *Human immortality.*

The contradiction between the mortal lot of the faithful and their confidence in God is not surmounted in the piety of the Old Testament.   Even to-day we cannot prove that human existence persists after the death of the body.   The supposition that the human soul possesses in itself the power of indestructible life is neither Biblical (1 Tim. vi. 16) nor deducible from what we know of the soul.   Science takes no cognizance of soul at all.   It can only establish particulars which we distinguish from movements in space as movements of the consciousness.   We call these, therefore, inward transactions.   As to whether in their totality they combine to form that living entity we call a soul we have no knowledge.   But we do know well that they are accompanied and conditioned, as they arise, by movements in space, in the first instance in our own body.   Hence it obviously follows that where the body breaks up the phenomena of consciousness become likewise imperceptible. The idea that after the death of the body the soul lives on as an intrinsically immortal entity, is not Biblical but Platonic, and it stands in opposition to the fact that the inner phenomena of consciousness are, in a manner beyond our ken, conditioned by the changes in the bodily organism. The solemn reality of death or the consciousness of the actual transience of our earthly life must have laid hold upon us as it laid hold upon the writers of the Old Testament, before we can grasp the wonderful power which does in fact lift us above death. The Christian thought of immortality does not express a conclusion to which every thinking man must come, but a fact which certain people experience in their faith in God. But to us Christians at any rate it must be clear that the continued existence of living religion is impossible in association with the idea that man will be annihilated at death. Nor is it difficult to show how confidence in an imperishable life becomes an essential element in our faith.

There is to be found in the Old Testament even in Israel's classical period the ancient idea of a shadow-existence in the realm of the dead, destitute of all hope; but even there it stands already in sharp opposition to that devotion to Almighty God which makes itself heard in the Old Testament. Such a faith always means an awakening to real life, and in the end it will always create the certainty that this life cannot cease to be; for assuredly we cannot think of a being that is really embraced by God's fatherly love as destined to annihilation in God's world. Jesus gives expression to this thought when in his answer to the Sadducees he bases man's immortality upon the fact that God is not the God of the dead but of the living (Luke xx. 38).

We cannot suppose, however, that the imperishable life of which we must be conscious in faith could be realized without a body. For we know that the fellowship with God for which we are destined and which means our eternal life is not possible apart from fellowship with other persons of God's making (Matt. xxii. 39). Since, however, we can have intercourse with such persons only through the medium of that external life which expresses us—only, that is to say, through a body—faith comes to hope not only for the immortality of the soul, but also for an imperishable human life in a body more perfect than this present one (1 Cor. xv. 35–50).

But a serious man will only be able to endure the thought of his own immortality if he has become conscious in himself of the beginnings of a life which does not grow old. Such an inexhaustible life, however, is open to us only in the knowledge of faith, and in fellowship with other persons, based upon loving service (1 Cor. xiii. 8). Wherefore our faith stamps as true the thought that we are to find again beyond death the imperishable element in the people we really love.

We look in vain for proofs of the immortality of the human individual. But we should stoutly contend for the position that we can enjoy here and now in our own souls the realization of the beginnings of an inexhaustible life. When this becomes for us an

undoubted fact, it inevitably produces a confidence
that we are in the hands of a life-force which will
overcome the death that is our lot in the world
(1 Cor. xv. 21, 55).

### 36. *The Goal of Man.*

The thought that the apparently infinite plurality of
the world is yet a whole under the dominion of God
is fortified in us by our attainment of the point of
view corresponding with it. This we possess through
experiencing in our own faith the beginnings of that
which we apprehend to be the eternal goal of all
mankind. If we become conscious of the reality of
God through the awakening in us of pure confidence,
that carries with it, too, a knowledge of the goal to
which God would lead us. God will one day bring
mankind to a perfect fellowship in which each individual will find inexhaustible tasks and infinite
increase of his personal life. This is the only reason
why the commandment to love one's neighbor,
which makes such a pure fellowship of love among
men our supreme aim, can stand side by side with the
commandment to love God. Because we are confident
that through God's almighty working we are being
brought to this goal which we have in view, we can
regard the seemingly illimitable conditions of our
existence as means to this end, and therefore as form-
ing a real cosmos.

This teleological origin of the idea of a universe is
misunderstood by pantheism, which unquestionably
does not possess that scientific foundation of which it
is wont to boast, and which, though its intention is

quite the contrary, is bound to work against religion and morality. But a similar mistake underlies, too, the orthodox assertion that there is a rational foundation for the idea of a divine Providence which co-ordinates the world into one wisely ordered whole; and the same applies to all the theologians' and philosophers' attempts at a theodicy.

### 37. *The revelations of the holiness of God within the, limits of our religious knowledge.*

Our conceptions of the divine attributes express the way in which faith recognizes God's working. We have no right to distinguish from this, as did the older dogmatics, a knowledge of God's nature. The conceptions whereby the older theology proposed to apprehend God's nature are un-Biblical, and have no value for faith. But even the modes of God's revealed working cannot yield us a uniform conception of his nature; for they contradict one another in a way that baffles us. As we gain conscious experience of the righteousness and goodness of God which inwardly constrain us, we arrive beyond doubt at the idea of a personal Spirit which in the depths of its life is understood by us and understands us. Only when such a communion with God becomes an indubitable reality to us can religion open the way to the fulfilment of our own life. But as trust in God produces in us the concept of his omnipotence, our idea of God's personality necessarily grows dim; for an Almighty Being cannot possess either the knowledge or the will by which we recognize personal life. An omnipotent Power is for us a quite inconceivable mystery. Therefore not only must we say to others that we cannot prove to them God's reality, but our own faith has to confess that for it, too, God lives in light unapproachable. None the less, the contention of pantheism that we must, therefore, give up the idea of God's personality is still mistaken (Dr. F. Strauss, *Glaubenslehre,* Bk. I., p. 504). Although the idea of omnipotence cannot be reconciled with our conception of personal life, we still see that the absolute confidence created in us implies both these ideas. It is when we consider the wonderful fact of that real life created and stirring in us that God Almighty is revealed to us as personal Spirit.

Nevertheless, the logical contradiction of the two ideas remains. Yet it cannot destroy the fact which is a matter of personal experience. It is only necessary that we should constantly be realizing that Power which, as our own experience testifies, produces absolute confidence in us. Moreover, the logical contradiction of those thoughts renders us the service of deepening our knowledge of God in one respect— in that it makes it clear that, though we may approach God more nearly, we can never touch him. God remains hidden to us even when he is near us. Our knowledge of God, then, can never be other than the clear knowledge of an activity which produces the stirrings of real life in us. But the Power to which we owe these experiences remains to us unknown.

Biblical piety defends itself against the mysticism which misunderstands this fact by its conception of the holiness—that is to say, the inviolable majesty—

of God. In the Old Testament God is called holy because he is exalted as the Supreme over all that is, because it is his will to be acknowledged as the Rock of a particular people (1 Sam. ii. 2), and because he withdraws himself from every approach of which he is not the initiator (1 Sam. vi. 20). This thought of God's strictly maintained isolation seems to fall into the background in the New Testament, where God breaks through every barrier between himself and us by the sacrifice of Jesus (Rom. viii. 32). But on the other side stand such sayings as John xvii. 11, the title πατερ αγιε, and the first petition of the Lord's Prayer. Particularly characteristic is the usage of the New Testament in referring to God, in the special sense of the Spirit imparting himself to the redeemed, as Holy Spirit. As a matter of fact the idea of God's holiness is not only maintained in the New Testament but even intensified; for particular stress is laid upon the fact that God even in his most intimate communion with man remains the Holy One. We are thus made to realize that for the creature God in himself is unapproachable. Free access to himself he will vouchsafe us only through the fact of his gift to us in the manifestation of Jesus (Matt. xi. 27; John xiv. 5–6; Heb. x. 20); and those to whose hearts he really comes near he thereby separates from the world or makes holy (Rom. xii. 2). The idea of holiness must, however, be found in some form or other in every real religion; for the religious man knows that his consciousness of God arises not on the basis of that which any man can establish for himself, but only in virtue of God's special working upon him.

# THE OVERCOMING OF SIN THROUGH FAITH WHICH IS GOD'S GIFT

## CHAPTER VIII

## SIN AND ITS CONSEQUENCES

38. *The knowledge of the nature of sin involved in faith.*

Religion universally regards sin as that which separates man from God and blessedness. Man can only recognize the fact of such sin when he has arrived at some understanding of that which alone can make him blessed, the rule of God in his heart. This separation from God he may then ascribe to another power which has set itself between him and God. But the notion that a creature such as the devil can bar the way of the seeker after God must ultimately be rendered impossible by the religious knowledge of God's omnipotence. He who has in him the elements of real religion dare not seek for an explanation of his sin outside himself. Rather he is constantly aware of the fact that it is his own sin which separates him from God. It is true that Jesus shared in the idea of a devil, as he did in general in the whole world-view

then current in Israel. He uses the idea of the devil
to illuminate the manner in which sin rules in the
world; but, on the other hand, he saw that sin has its
origin in the will or in the heart of man (Matt. xii.
34-35; xv. 19). He sought, then, simply to present
us with the fact of our own sin. But when we recognize sin to be our own free act, it becomes incomprehensible to us. That it is, nevertheless, a reality which
must needs rob every man of his peace is presupposed
by Jesus and corroborated by our own experiences.
The reality of sin in us and around us becomes more
manifest to us in proportion as we gain more clarity
and freedom in our moral life. Where there is inward
growth in man the consciousness of sin's reality
becomes deeper.

But our idea of the nature of sin is also dependent
upon the depth of our religious and ethical understanding. In the Old Testament sin is still sometimes
regarded as the transgression of commandments whose
justification is hidden from men. In the Christian
community, on the other hand, a man should know
for himself what sin is and why it is sin; for Christian
faith has attained to the knowledge that a man can
only be in fellowship with God as he is inwardly submissive to him. But this only happens when he trusts
in God alone and seeks to make his whole life a service
of his neighbor, thus fulfilling the command to love
God and one's neighbor. He is, therefore, bound to
regard nothing as sin save a disposition to actions
which are devoid of faith and love. Lack of faith
and selfishness are sins, and these alone.

### 39. *The initial form of sin.*

To comprehend the origin of sin is impossible to us. The Biblical story of the Fall cannot help us; yet we can and must make clear to ourselves the primary form of sin. The spiritual attitude in which unbelief and selfishness are as yet only implicit, but which is already in every case an indication of insincerity, is devotion to the pleasures of sense, or sloth. Under the rule of God there should be formed in us God's image, that is, the power of a love which through self-denial creates something new. This work of God is checked in us by the slothful devotion to pleasures of sense. So long as this does not make us conscious of opposition to God and the good, we have to do not only with a *fomes peccati*, as the Roman Church teaches, but also with sin in its initial form. This must ultimately issue in unbelief and selfishness; for since we are hindered on the road to inward independence through the enjoyment of such pleasures, we become godless and loveless.

Paul speaks of this primary form of sin in his teaching about the σαρξ. In the Old Testament man is called flesh to indicate his impotence and ephemeral nature in contrast with God Almighty. Paul, on the other hand, uses this same word to indicate that man is hindered by his natural life from arriving at the power and liberty of real faith and of a loving will (Rom. vii. 18; viii. 6). In the flesh he sees the work of a power which actually compels man to sin (Gal. v. 16–21; Rom. viii. 5–8). Therefore Paul calls sin simply works of the flesh (Gal. v. 19 f.). Nevertheless, one

cannot say that Paul regards the life of the senses as
the cause of sin; for were that the case Paul would
regard the task of morality as the mortification of this
sensual life. But he undoubtedly finds the task of
morality in loyalty to our God-given vocation and in
the love of our neighbor. Indeed, he fought against
that ascetic morality which would do away with the
life of sense as itself a work of the flesh (Cor. ii. 16–
23). When, therefore, Paul says that sin originates in
the instincts of the natural life, he does not go so far as
to say that these forces are intrinsically evil. He means,
rather, that man's natural life, the instincts of which
are felt to be imperative, becomes a source of sin
when a man loses inner communion with God and thus
the power to win control over these natural forces.
Paul's teaching about the σαρξ is, therefore, not intended to explain the origin of sin, which for the
Apostle, too, remains an inexplicable falling away of
the creature from its Creator (Rom. v. 12; 2 Cor.
xi. 3). Paul rather seeks to indicate that sin in its
beginnings as the spirit's indulgence of the sensual life,
a thing not intrinsically evil, looks harmless enough;
but the ultimate issue of this enervating sloth is sin in
its supreme form. It is precisely because the motions
of the sensual instincts are not intrinsically evil that
they can be perilous to us. They deceive us as soon
as we carelessly surrender ourselves to them. If we
do not keep them in control they become in us a
power which leads us into sin (Rom. vii. 22–24). It is
therefore of the greatest practical importance for every
one of us in regard to sin that we should not only keep
clearly in view its final issue in unbelief and loveless-

ness, but should also appraise it as sin in its initial form.

### 40. *Guilt.*

By faith we realize not only the essence of sin and its primary form, but also its present reality in ourselves. When the God of the Scriptures reveals himself to us we perceive in ourselves and around us a dominion of sin. We do not, then, obtain a clear view of the reality of sin primarily from our moral knowledge, but only from the unveiling to us of God's reality. It is only when in our experience of God's revelation of himself we realize the power of the holy that we see clearly our own uncleanness and impotence. All those to whom God reveals himself are of one mind in their consciousness of the universal sinfulness of humanity as expressed in Scripture. But this is only to recognize the empirical fact of the universal sway of sin; nothing has been said as to its necessity. In Scripture, however, the consciousness of sin is closely bound up with the thought of guilt, and this is borne out by our own experience.

According to our belief man, however debased he may be, is yet a free being, because it is God's will to be his father, and God can enter into fellowship only with those who have a real inner life and are free persons. No less firmly is the thought of our freedom grounded upon the moral consciousness which recognizes the absolute validity of the moral law. We are therefore bound to trace the fact of sin in ourselves and others back to the free choice of the will against God, who is the living power of the good. It is this responsibility of man for his sinful state that we call his guilt.

In dealing with the idea of guilt, however, there is always a second element to be considered. We also use the word "guilt" to denote the relation of the sinner to the Power which he has wronged by his transgression of the law. Thus when we speak of guilt in the field of jurisprudence we mean that through some action the impersonal power of the State has suffered injury. Punishment must consequently be inflicted to restore the disturbed order. Guilt, understood in this sense, is to be taken as removed when punishment is executed, or when by an act of grace on the part of the authority it is remitted. But the situation is entirely different when a man recognizes his action as a transgression of the moral law or of God's commandment. The moral consciousness which thus confirms the truth of the moral law carries within itself the inevitable necessity of self-condemnation, and thus forestalls the need of any external judgment. This sense of guilt felt by the moral consciousness is, however, still more intensified when we realize that our sin has caused an inward separation between us and those who are dear to us. This applies with special force to the relation between the religious man and his God. We dare no longer put our confidence in God when we have to confess to ourselves that our disposition and mode of life are out of harmony with his almighty will. It is the realization of the impossibility of friendship with God that creates in us the religious consciousness of guilt. Obviously we cannot be quit of this burden of guilt by any effort for our

own betterment; for the sense of guilt before God
will paralyze our courage to start a new life. The
sinner experiences the fact of the rejection of God in
the inward constraint that forces him to write his own
condemnation. The power of truth is the power of
God.

### 41. *The corporate sin of human society and inherited sin.*

In the self-judgment involved in the sense of guilt
the Christian experiences a sense of God's separation
from him. The inner enfeeblement which follows
makes the beginning of a new life impossible for him.
This dominion of sin becomes still clearer to him by
reason of the fact that experience shows that not only
does sin appear in every individual (Matt. vii. 11;
Rom. iii. 10; iii. 23), but it also rules in human society,
whence the individual springs.

Through our sins we all help to make the fellowship
and organization of society sinful. All the members
of society are responsible for the sin which thus arises.
It is, therefore, corporate sin. Hence the sin of the
individual can never be distinguished with certainty
from the sin of the human society to which he belongs.
But from the corporate sin of human society there
issues also its inevitable inheritance. Every man is
influenced by the corporate sin of earlier generations
without the possibility of defence against it; for it
is only through being brought up in human society
that we become men. Now all education begins with
a child's accepting the ideas and the behavior of
adult persons. But if these spiritual instruments of

education have been spoiled by sin, we imbibe sin in
the course of our education. If there should anywhere
appear a human being devoid of this sinful attitude,
he would immediately and inevitably be felt to constitute a new beginning in the whole historical life of
mankind.

These considerations bring home to the modern man
the inevitable necessity of the inheritance of sin more
forcibly than did the idea which has dominated the
Church since Augustine, though it is incapable of
demonstration, that sin is inherited by the mere fact
of physical descent from parents. It is, therefore, a
mistake to suppose that the idea of original sin has
become unthinkable to the modern mind. On the
contrary, this idea has become much more intelligible
than before to all who recognize at all the reality of
sin amongst men. Still, we can no longer give Augustine's answer to the question of how man can be
responsible for inherited sin. The Reformers no less
than the Roman Church taught that all people who
are not redeemed by Christ must be subject to damnation because they have all sinned in Adam. This
basis of responsibility for original sin we must reject,
not only because proof of it was sought in the false
translation of Rom. v. 12 (*in quo omnes peccaverunt*),
but rather because we see that we cannot be condemned because of the action of another over whom
we had no control. Accordingly we cannot conceive
that God will condemn us for this reason.

Now Schleiermacher and Ritschl supposed that a
substitute for the idea of original sin, which is burdened
with insoluble contradictions, could and must be found

in the idea of corporate sin. The individual could not, to be sure, isolate himself from the corporate sin of human society; but his participation in this corporate sin was always realized by his own personal actions; for that reason everyone is involved in responsibility for it. This is true, however, only of the relation of the adult to the sinful conditions of the society in which he lives. On the other hand, everyone has been subject from infancy to the corrupting influence of earlier generations. Obviously, therefore, before he could participate in the corporate sin of society as at present constituted, he was involved in a perverted mode of thought and volition. So the question again arises as to how a man can be held responsible for this inherited corruption, from which all his sinful actions are obviously seen to issue.

The Reformers were, nevertheless, right in their firm adherence to the view that sin so inherited is to be regarded as sin in the full sense of the term. It is not to be conceived simply as a disease, as Zwingli thought, but as the personal action of the man who thereby becomes sinful (*Conf. ii., Apol. i.*). It must, indeed, be granted that when we judge man's sinful condition to be inherited we do not deduce his own responsibility for this corruption; but it is none the less certain that the man who has attained to ripe ethical knowledge, and hence to the consciousness of his freedom, regards as his own act all his ethical relations. Thus the fact of the matter is obviously this: that every individual is inevitably bound to be sinful from the beginning of his conscious life, and is equally bound to condemn himself for his sin as soon as his knowledge of the

moral law creates in him the consciousness of freedom.
The incomprehensible thing in all this, however, is not
the fact of the inheriting of corruption, but the free
will which, in spite of a man's dependence upon sinful
humanity, assumes responsibility for his disharmony
with the moral law.

### 42. *Judgment.*

The judgment or punishment of sin is executed even
in the earthly life of the sinner: (1) in the inward
compulsion to condemn himself, (2) in the knowledge
that it is impossible for him to deliver himself from
sin through his own efforts, (3) in the way in which the
sinner reacts to his lot in life.   But if God has revealed
himself to a man, he sees in those experiences which
render him impotent and miserable the power of the
God from whom he knows himself inwardly separated
and by whom abandoned to perdition.   The sinner's
faith in God is then transformed into fear of the judgment or of the wrath of God.   If then the sinner filled
with this fear recognizes at the same time through
faith that God would have him a free being who should
therefore work out a destiny for himself, he must
expect that in God's judgment there will be realized
the issues of that tendency to sin of which he cannot
rid himself.   The Christian cannot, therefore, think of
the ultimate punishment as anything arbitrary, but as
the full realization of the operation of sin itself (Gal.
vi. 7-8).   The completed punishment of sin is, fundamentally, sin in its completion—namely, a life actually
lived for itself alone, or a life in utter isolation.   Herein
the tendency to selfishness or to lovelessness arrives at

its inevitable goal. This, then, is the future which
Christian faith unrolls before the eyes of a man when
it brings him to the knowledge of his sin. According
to the Synoptic Gospels Jesus himself characterized
this survival of the condemned in the outermost dark-
ness or in utter isolation as a thing without end.

In the moment when we suffer our fate as God's
retributive punishment, faith begins manifestly to
dissolve. The world-conquering power of faith is then
entirely destroyed by sin. For that reason we can no
longer hold to the truth of the Christian idea of God
himself (Matt. v. 44–45); for it is obviously impossible to find the God who loves his enemies in the God
who requites his enemies with endless pain.

## CHAPTER IX

# THE REDEMPTION THROUGH JESUS CHRIST

### 43. *The conception of redemption in the Christian Churches.*

In the ancient Church before Augustine the idea held sway from Irenæus onward that redemption recovers for the human race the power that issues in eternal life ($\alpha\phi\theta\alpha\rho\sigma\iota\alpha$), and that as a new law it is revealed to the individual man as the way to eternal life. This shape given to the idea of redemption moulded the form of the thought of Christ's divinity, as it is presented to us in the dogma of the Person of Christ developed at that time, that is, in the doctrine of the two natures united in him. In general, this view of redemption expressed what the Christian understood by redemption. It opens to him the way to real or eternal life. But what is meant by eternal life in the sense of the Gospels was not yet clearly grasped in this view. It had rightly been taught that redemption is accomplished by Jesus' entering into the history of mankind and linking us with God. But it had not yet been made clear that Jesus belongs to the historical life of mankind, not so much by his birth as by his work. Finally, in that early period of Church history redemption was described as a physical process which indeed renewed human nature but left untouched the inner life of the individual. Redemption from sin was only considered in so far as it was supposed that man could be rid of sin through the new, perfect law given through Christ.

It was the task of later development, in which the Eastern Church took no further share, to fill up the deficiencies in the early Church conception of redemption. In the Western Church alone Augustine established the recognition that redemption must be concerned with the emancipation of individuals from sin, since the power of sin makes the fulfilment of God's law impossible for them (1 Peter ii. 24). Therefore in the Roman Church we meet with a very lively desire to find liberation from sin and its consequences in the Church, which is the Redeemer's work. But here it remained obscure how such ethical renewal is accomplished as an inward transaction in the consciousness of the sinner. Consequently it also passed unnoticed that the New Testament community knew itself to be in enjoyment of redemption, although it remained aware of the continuance of sin in its midst. Yet if in the New Testament the man who is already redeemed is again and again required to put away sin, the immediate consequence of redemption cannot be regarded as a magical liberation from sin.

It was in the Reformation that the task of supplementing these deficiencies was begun. The Reformers, with Augustine, saw the goal of redemption in the emancipation of the individual from the power of sin. But they also recovered a further element of New Testament knowledge, namely, as to the manner in which the decisive transformation takes place in the inner life of sinful men. They followed the conception which we find in Jesus and in Paul that the sinner is saved by faith. Redemption consists in the revival in man of the faith which his sins had destroyed. Very soon, it is true, this idea in the evangelical Churches received a form which rendered almost unrecognizable the meaning of the New Testament proclamation of redemption by faith. None the less, Evangelical Christianity has never entirely lost sight of the recognition that the beginning of redemption lies in that transformation of our attitude to God which is brought about by the Redeemer. According to the Evangelical conception, then, redemption is primarily a religious matter, a recreation of the faith which sin has destroyed. It is accomplished in a communion between God and ourselves consciously experienced by us and mediated by the Redeemer. On the other hand, ethical emancipation, which makes inward freedom from sin possible to a man, is regarded as a consequence of this religious redemption. Thus the task of a theology which purports to develop the Reformers' work is to show how redemption so understood can be realized by us as a present experience, and how the beginning of a new life can thereby be given to us.

### 44. *The orthodox Protestant doctrine of Christ's redeeming work.*

The older Protestant theology sought to find a foundation for the certainty of redemption by assembling all the presumed teaching that it found in the New Testament about the past work of Jesus and about his present hidden working. Every individual should then say to himself that he must proceed to apply to his own case to-day all that according to this teaching Christ has done and is doing for the redemption of mankind. In the seventeenth century this was developed in accordance with the Reformers' accepted principles, in the doctrine of the *munus Christi triplex*. It was maintained that because Christ, according to 1 Tim. ii. 5, is the perfect Mediator, his work must combine the functions of the three Old Testament mediators between God and Man. Christ therefore assumed successively the three offices of Prophet, Priest, and King. On earth he worked first as Prophet, then as Priest; he now works as King, by ruling the world to the best advantage of his own.

Ritschl objected to this doctrine on the ground that the true mutual relationship of the three functions was here incorrectly represented. For Jesus' work upon his followers as Prophet and Priest contributes to the accomplishment of the work of the Messianic King, who is to realize God's rule upon earth. This kingly function, therefore, is the proper vocation of Christ. Yet he fulfils it not by force but by the spiritual means of the Prophet and the Priest. By this contention Ritschl remedied a fault in the historical conception. But in so doing he did not put his finger on the chief defect of Protestant orthodoxy, which lies in the fact that the doctrine which was to be arrived at in this way had been looked upon as constituting in itself the proper means of redemption. By adopting this doctrine of what Christ did in his life on earth and is secretly doing now man is redeemed.

This opinion obviously constitutes a grave hindrance to that which was recognized by the Reformers as the proper characteristic of the Christian—namely, the fact that he is certain of his salvation and in the power of this conviction gains courage to begin a new life. For no one can be made sure of his own redemption by hearing a doctrine of redemption and then endeavoring to hold it true and apply it to himself. An effort of this kind on man's part can never lead to inward freedom and transformation. This can only come to him through facts which he cannot choose but see confronting him, provided these same facts are potent enough to give a new content to his life. From his present plight the sinner can be saved only through the present working upon him of facts which he is not first obliged to force himself to accept as true and then apply to himself, since he already knows them in his own experience.

### 45. *The redeeming power of the Person of Jesus.*

That Jesus Christ has the power to redeem us can only mean that our present experience of the reality of his Person convinces us as nothing else does that God will accept us. Every other conception of Jesus' redeeming power would be inconsistent with the fundamental Christian principle that we are redeemed not by something that may be connected with his Person but by Jesus himself. It would also be inconsistent with the fundamental thought of Jesus' Gospel, that it is in God's rule in our hearts that our salvation consists.

We cannot experience redemption in a force issuing from Jesus, nor even in the present working of the exalted Lord; for every indefinite force eludes our experience, and similarly the work of the exalted Lord is hidden from us. We can be saved only by a reality presented to us as a fact of our own experience, a reality indubitable as our need. Consequently it is very possible that people who do not know Jesus himself may yet be inwardly near to him; but he can only redeem those who in meeting with him himself have realized the working of God upon them in such wise that they can no longer deny it. If he is our Redeemer we must have discovered in him that one thing which awakens pure love and pure fear in us, or which can have complete sway over our soul. But our redemption by this experience of the power of Jesus always depends upon whether we ourselves desire deliverance from sin; for we remain in the power of sin if we do not completely submit ourselves to the power that is manifested in Jesus, but try to withdraw ourselves from it. We recognized it to be an inevitable consequence of the sense of guilt that the sinner avoids all that brings God near to him— God whose judgment he fears. Hence the question arises how in spite of this circumstance it is possible for the power which touches us in the Person of Jesus to unite us to God, or how we receive through him the προσαγωγη προς τον θεον (the access to God) to which Paul testifies (Rom. v. 2; Eph. ii. 18; iii. 12).

46. *The redemption from sin which Jesus bestowed on his first disciples.*

How Jesus used his power over the heart of the sinner to help him is to be seen in the New Testament

most clearly in the story of the events in the house of
Simon the Pharisee, as related in Luke vii. 36–50
(cf. also Mark ii. 5). In the attitude of the woman
who thrust herself upon Jesus in the house of the
Pharisee two elements are to be distinguished: first, the
sinful woman shows herself to be profoundly moved,
even before Jesus has said a word to her. The mere
fact of Jesus' presence, that is to say, the impression of
his moral purity and vitality which she received from
his appearance, must have worked upon her as if she
were standing before her judge. Secondly, she none the
less receives courage to draw near to him. Obviously
she is confident that he will not at once thrust her from
him with loathing as other religious folk would do,
but will accept the tokens of her love. This is the
situation of which Jesus says in his conversation with
the Pharisee that her showing him such love is the
proof her sins are forgiven her. Only then does he
turn to the woman herself and say, "Thy sins are
forgiven thee; thy faith hath saved thee."

In this case the evidence that the forgiveness of sins
is an accomplished fact is to be sought first in this, that
the woman held fast to the fact which gave her courage
to seek help from Jesus, and then, secondly, that she had
the experience of actually not being thrust away by
him. As soon as she had approached him, she could
not do enough to show by her overflowing gratitude
that she had received that for which she had looked
to him; it was by the manner of his reception of her
that he helped her. But in all this Jesus did nothing
so far which the eye could see. It was the quiet
power of his Person which produced in the woman

profound penitence and therewith the courage to
approach him.  It appears to have pleased him that
she so turned to him for help and so expressed her
gratitude to him.  Thus he did what was to the
Pharisee a shocking thing—he did not reject her tokens
of love.

That the forgiveness of her sins had become for her
an indubitable fact was then stated by Jesus for the
benefit of the Pharisee, and illustrated by the case of
the two debtors.  It was because forgiveness had
brought her immediate happiness that the woman
showed him her grateful love.  She had not merely
heard an announcement that she was to be forgiven,
but had already received forgiveness in what had
passed; the significance of this is clear.  Forgiveness
consists simply in this, that the holy Power of moral
purity, from which she felt herself separated by a
wide gulf, did not in fact reject her.  Thereby Jesus
made her realize that she was of value to him.  But
this gave rise in her to the assurance that, since this
man does not cast her away, God himself would
accept her.  According to this story, then, to accept
God's forgiveness means that we become aware in a
fact of our experience that the same God who judges
as for our sins still seeks us to unite us with himself.

47. *The Orthodox Protestant doctrine of the attain-
      ment of God's forgiveness through the redeem-
      ing work of Christ (his priestly office).*

In the orthodox doctrine of the *munus Christi
triplex* the largest place is occupied by the doctrine of
the priestly office or the doctrine of redemption.  Its

purpose is to find for the Christian a basis for the
assurance of his redemption. To this end the view is
expounded that Christ accomplished redemption by a
double exercise of his obedience: (1) through his
*obedientia activa* or through his deeds; (2) through his
*obedientia passiva* or through his Passion. In his deeds
he perfectly fulfilled God's law. Since, however, in
virtue of his divine nature he himself was under no
obligation to fulfil the law, this exercise of his obedience may be applied to the benefit of us sinners. Then
in his Passion he took on himself all due to mankind
for sin, and suffered the punishment of eternal damnation in his dereliction on the cross. Since, however, he
himself had not deserved any punishment, his Passion
may be accepted by God in lieu of the punishment of
sin, that is, in lieu of the eternal damnation of all
mankind. Consequently God can now give rein to his
mercy toward sinners because the requirements of his
justice upon them are satisfied. According to Paul's
doctrine (2 Cor. v. 18) sinners become reconciled to
God through the convincing proof of God's love. God
is not the object but the subject of the *katallassein*.
According to this doctrine, on the other hand, God is
reconciled by the sacrifice offered to him. The satisfaction offered by Christ to the righteous God in place
of the sinner (*satisfactio vicaria*) should therefore be
the basis of our confidence in God's forgiveness, as
soon as we accept the idea or believe that the work of
Jesus as the God-man must have such a value for God
that his wrath may thereby be allayed.

This doctrine affords no answer to the Christian's
question as to how he can become personally certain

of his own redemption; all that it attempts to do is to show how in general it has become possible for God to forgive sinners. But even if this were capable of proof and had been proved in this way, that would be no help to any one of us; for a Christian's longing for salvation does not aim at certainty as to how God's forgiveness of sins is possible in general. What he desires is the assurance that by some incomprehensible act of God's grace he himself is actually forgiven. Such an assurance cannot come to us through any doctrine which we are prepared to accept, but only through a fact which is rooted in our own life as a working of God that we have ourselves experienced.

But the thought that Christ took our place as substitute will, it is true, subsequently arise in the man who is already redeemed by Christ. It is to be found in the New Testament chiefly where Christ is compared with the suffering Servant of God in Isa. liii, and probably in the passage Rom. iii. 25–26. But this thought can be a truth only for those who have already received the forgiveness of God through Christ. They then say: what *we* should have done and suffered *He* has done and suffered for us. To them this thought serves as a bulwark of their assurance of forgiveness, as against the doubt which again and again arises from the sense of guilt. But we must guard against the mistake of supposing that forgiveness itself is won for a man by his taking over from a Christian who has been forgiven this notion of Christ's significance as a substitute; for this idea can only be grasped in its real meaning and truth when one already possesses the assurance of forgiveness. A sinner can become certain

of the forgiveness of his sins only by an actual experi‑
ence of forgiveness, not by an imaginative grasp of its
possibility.

48. *The forgiveness of sins, which we may obtain now
through the power of the Person of Jesus.*

The doctrine of reconciliation in Protestant ortho‑
doxy maintains that God's will to redeem sinners could
only overcome the opposition in God's own nature in
virtue of the work of Jesus. Thus a reconciliation was
reached between God's mercy or goodness and his
justice (*temperamentum justitiæ et misericordiæ*). In
this way the idea arose that God is reconciled by the
work of Christ because the requirements of his justice
were thereby satisfied or his wrath appeased. Such a
conception, however, is entirely un-Biblical. For, in
the first place, the work of Jesus is not to reconcile
God, but is the result of God's own working in order
to reconcile sinners (2 Cor. v. 18). In the second place
it is a fundamental conception of Biblical piety that
God's goodness comes to meet every sinner who would
return to him. This unlimited, indestructible goodness
of God towards everyone in whom there is still any
trace of longing for him Jesus depicts both in the
parable of the Prodigal Son (Luke xv.) and also when
he bases the command to love one's enemies upon
God's own attitude towards his enemies (Matt. v.
45). For Jesus himself, therefore, it must have been
inconceivable that his work was necessary to effect a
change in God's attitude to sinners.

On the contrary, Jesus clearly meant that for certain
men the assurance of God's forgiveness was made

possible through himself alone—through his explicitly conveying to them the forgiveness of their sins. He must, therefore, have seen that only through his working upon them could the goodness of God open these men's eyes to forgiveness as a matter of their own experience. Only by the power of his Person upon their heart could God's goodness working upon them become an emancipating experience. But this happened because the living unity in God of justice and goodness, which for their part they felt to be a contradiction, stood visibly before their eyes in the Person of Jesus. This came about when they felt themselves utterly humbled and at the same time exalted by him to the courage required to begin a new life. If then we too are to receive God's forgiveness through Christ, this is assuredly rendered possible only by our coming to know him, experiencing his power over us, and so becoming aware how that power at once condemns our sins and stirs in us courage to start a new life.

True, the Person of Jesus is no longer present to our senses as was the case with the first disciples, so that we may have sensible proof of his goodness directed to us in particular. None the less, we, like them, can receive God's forgiveness through our own experience of the power of the Person of Jesus. We, like the first disciples, owe our experience of this redeeming power solely to the fact that for us also Jesus is the perfect manifestation of the only One to whom we can know ourselves completely subject. This most powerful experience of God's working upon us, however, only becomes the experience of forgiveness when at the same time we picture to ourselves Jesus' death on the cross.

According to the tradition of the New Testament
Jesus ultimately won his way through to an acceptance
of death at the hands of his enemies as something
belonging to his calling, something laid upon him by
God. When we have found God in Christ, the trustworthiness of this tradition will be established for us
by something which we need not learn first from the
tradition, since we can see it for ourselves. It is absolutely clear to us that Jesus could only remain what he
had become to his own by refusing to retreat before
his enemies. Only so was his power to bring other
men to God saved from destruction. It would have
vanished had Jesus allowed his disciples to get the
impression that he had withdrawn before the power
of evil. It was necessary therefore that, so far from
shunning a dangerous conflict with his adversaries, he
should oppose them openly and incite their hatred
to the highest pitch. The doom which this involved
for him could not remain hidden from him. He must,
then, have gone to meet this danger because it was
plain to him that God required of him that he should
not flee from it. He saw that only in this way could
he maintain that unity with God through which alone
he had the power to redeem men at their point of
deepest need.

That the willing surrender of his life to this death
was the means required by God to bring help to sinful
men Jesus ultimately expressed in peculiarly explicit
terms at the Last Supper with his disciples. Beyond
doubt it is only because in such a way Jesus indelibly
impressed upon the minds of his disciples that it was
for our sakes that he took upon himself the death of

the cross, that we can find in him the utterly convincing expression of God's forgiveness. Otherwise we could not put away the thought that Jesus shrank back before such a power of evil as is disclosed in our own hearts by our consciousness of guilt. It was his cross that first brought home to his community the assurance that he was ready to do and suffer anything for those who had begun to feel in his Person the heart-constraining power of God. But in the cross such men always see the complete manifestation of the fact of God's desire to say to them that their guilt, however grievous it be, shall not separate them from him. This is the forgiveness of God which we experience. Doubtless it contradicts the judgment of our sense of guilt that God will and must reject us; yet it becomes a matter of certainty to us because that very power of the Holy One whereby we feel ourselves condemned reveals itself to us—in an indisputable fact—as a love which takes the heaviest burden on its heart to prevent our perishing in the terror of our sense of guilt. When we find God's forgiveness, then, in the fact that Christ is given to us, we know by experience that God's love is mightier than our heart filled with its sense of guilt (1 John iii. 20), and we are then in a position to understand the meaning and truth of the conception, rightly treasured in the Church's doctrine of the Atonement, that Christ for our salvation answers for us. He answers for us against those doubts and accusations which God allows our bad conscience to breed in us. If we do not live through these accusations and overcome them in our hearts, we do not win free from sin. The Reformers' doctrine of justification based on

Pauline teaching explains why this experience of the forgiveness of God is to be understood as the sinner's redemption.  (Cf. § 51.)

### 49. *The Resurrection of Jesus.*

1 Cor. xv. gives us the first certain testimony to the appearances of Jesus to his disciples after his death. This is the standard by which we must judge the trustworthiness of the narratives given in the Gospels. From these latter stories we can no longer divine with certainty what the original happenings were, but they indicate the value which the appearances recorded by Paul had for the first disciples.  Only the appearance of the Crucified to them as a living presence made his death actually a redemption in their eyes.  True, there had earlier been created in them the confidence that Jesus was their Redeemer.  One may not say, therefore, that their faith first found its basis in these appearances; but it is manifest that it was these which preserved their faith from shipwreck.

According to the New Testament the Risen Christ never appeared to others as he did to those who were already united with him by inextinguishable memories. But these disciples were bound to say to themselves subsequently that even without any such appearances what they had previously learnt ought to have assured them that for Jesus his death was the completion, not the negation, of his obedience, and was so far a victory (Luke xxiv. 25–26; John xx. 29; Phil. ii. 8).  But actually it was only under the impression of these wonderful appearances that the idea which they had previously accepted regained its power—that the Man who had become for them the pledge of God's love could not be conceived as perishing in the world, and that nothing could separate them from him (John x. 28 f.).

The same is true of ourselves. Our assurance that Jesus is alive and is not separated from us is not primarily based upon a report of events such as these; for it is already implicit in the faith created and maintained in us by the power of Jesus, under whose influence we stand. For a firm faith it would, of course, be self-evident that Jesus cannot have perished in death and departed from us; but in our own case also we observe that which occurred with the first disciples. They needed the help of the appearances which they saw. To us, indeed, this experience is not vouchsafed; but we experience divine help in the fact that the Christian community arose as it did. For our faith recognizes from this that God has allowed those events to happen which had to happen if it were to be possible for us also to come to know Jesus and so experience his redeeming power. Our faith can only come to its full strength if in our hearts the confidence arises that Jesus does not belong to the dead, but is living in the power of God (Rom. x. 9). Our confidence, too, that God does not allow us to perish in death is fortified by the fact that we see our own experience of the power of the Person of Jesus giving birth to the thought that he is alive. But such a confidence could not rise in our own hearts if we had not come beforehand to know Jesus and to experience his power. Therefore the events by which the faith of the first disciples was saved from shipwreck have imperishable importance for the Christian community in every age. If they had not occurred we should not have received the witness of the earliest communities to Jesus' life on earth. If the picture of Jesus there given us is for us the means of our salvation, then also in the events upon which the disciples built after the death of Jesus we see works of God for our salvation. That, then, is the content of the Easter message of which we can be well assured as a fact on which our faith is based; for that alone presents itself to us as a matter of our own experience. On the other hand, the experience of the first disciples at that time is not vouchsafed to us, and there is no historical proof that can make it completely certain to us. In Christian preaching, therefore, the Scripture story of Easter can only be used in such a way as to point the congregation to that which alone can create faith in its members. Christian preaching must confine itself strictly to that which is presented to it as indubitable fact. If we accept such fact as God's gift to us, this real obedience of faith will help us then to have unqualified joy even in the narratives of the appearances of the Risen Lord (contradictory and obscure though they are to the historian), and of his communion with the disciples. It will then be enough for us that this at any rate was the way in which the picture of these events established itself in the minds of those men who, as the first generation of a new humanity, lived in the power of the Person of Jesus. The fact that what happened at that time remains by God's will veiled from us will then cease to trouble us.

50. *The exalted Lord.*

If our hearts are convinced on the basis of personal experience that Christ cannot have remained in the grasp of death—are convinced, that is to say, that he is alive and present—then we have also grasped the conception that Christ is still active in the work to which he was called.  For to him as Redeemer to cease to do a Redeemer's work would spell not continuance of life but loss of it.  True, he can now no longer bring us God's revelation, for he himself is hidden from our eyes.  Thus we can only conceive of the continuance of his work for us in this sense—that as a hidden Power he exercises a redeeming influence upon our life. Ultimately, therefore, the faith which the historical Christ creates in us gives rise to the thought that for the consummation of his work in us he now holds secret sway over our destinies, to the end that we may therein have richer experience of his consolation and prove more determined followers of him.

If, then, it becomes possible for us to accept everything that falls to our lot as a work of the love of Jesus which is revealed to us in his historical life, then Jesus has thereby established in us that rule of God which as Messiah he was to bring to men.  If in everything we depend upon we experience the power of this love that educates us, then God is ruling in us as he desires to rule.  To give us this picture of the God who works upon us, Jesus in his preaching used the image of the Father; but the working of an almighty love becomes more evident to us once the conviction has been created in us that the whole reality in the midst of which we are placed has been fashioned by the fixed purpose of Jesus never to forsake us. That the conviction of the resurrection of Jesus really lives in our faith is evident to us not in our willingness to accept as veritable history the New Testament accounts of the communion of the first disciples with the Risen Lord, but in the fact that we are now really able to interpret the story of our own life as his dealing with us.

Our faith attains its fulfilment in the assurance that the meaning and purpose of the living Person of Jesus is supreme in the infinite reality that surrounds us. In this we possess the redemption which within the limits of our earthly experience we are capable of experiencing. Our faith in the exalted Lord is, therefore, the consummation of the salvation of man upon earth. Herein we receive from Christ not only reconciliation with the God revealed to us in him, but also the assurance that he surrounds us with secret powers of redemption; and finally we receive the clear view of the life to come in which lies our eternal goal. Beyond these things we can only wait for the redemption of our body —that is to say, for the time when the conditions of our existence will be so changed that the faith of men who have yet to overcome passes over into the vision of those who have won the victory (2 Cor. v. 6 f.).

51. *The assurance of salvation in the consciousness of justification by faith.*

Jesus' thought that God's rule in us is our redemption Paul expressed in very different terms. For the most part he says that he knows himself set free by the spirit of God or Christ from everything that destroyed his blessedness. The longest exposition of this kind occurs in Rom. viii, particularly in verses 2, 9, 15, and 26. But in the few passages in which Paul defines his position as against the Pharisees he entirely transforms his opponents' conception of a justification through God, and in this new form employs it to express the Christian assurance of salvation.

The Pharisees believed that the Kingdom of God would come to them in consequence of their righteousness because God would justify them or recognize them as belonging to him in virtue of their good works. In opposition to this Paul explains in his letters to the Romans and to the Galatians that man cannot through his good works have the assurance of belonging to God. He can be certain of his salvation only by keeping before his eyes the fact of God's grace directed towards him. This, however, happens in faith or in trust in Jesus Christ; for herein it becomes clear to the sinner that in spite of his sins God treats him as his child. Consequently it is not the righteous who will be declared righteous, but the sinners in whom God, working on them through Christ, creates trust in his mercy. Thus the sinner who knows himself otherwise separated from God by his guilt is led to God through a fact of his own experience.

Paul, therefore, only uses the term "justification before God" because his opponents whom he wished to refute conceived of redemption as a legal transaction between God and the sinner. When, on the other hand, it is not in his mind to refute this notion of the Pharisees, he uses the simpler expressions which suit the religious aspect of redemption. None the less, the idea of the justification of the sinner still holds a special importance for us, because the Reformers later expressed in this form their controversy with the Roman Church. Luther, however, did not do this so often as is sometimes supposed on the basis of his statement in the *A.S.* ii. Art. 1. But since this form was used in the *Confessio Augustana,* Art. 4, and most fundamentally in the second and third articles of the Apology, soon the whole of Protestantism came to express the Christian's assurance of salvation in this form.

According to the doctrine of the Reformers justification is a judgment of God upon the sinner, whereby God says to him: "Thou art fit for communion with me." This hits off correctly in general terms the Pauline notion of justification. The word *iustificatus,* which may have several meanings, is then more exactly defined by the words *a Deo acceptus,* and the *iustificare* of this action of God is made to coincide with the *peccata remittere.* The Reformers, however, thought themselves faced with the question how the sinner may appropriate or apply to himself this judgment of God. This indicates a confusion originating in their Catholic past. For as soon as the thought occurs to the mind that the sinner may and should become aware of the judgment of God's grace upon his soul, there is no point in going on to ask how we can succeed in applying this judgment to our own case. For it is only as a message of God to ourselves that we become aware of it. It is, however, quite otherwise if we are unable to find the ground of our assurance of salvation in what is said to us by God himself, but are content instead to allow ourselves to be put off with the possibility of God's grace to sinners. In that case we must at least seek to attain to the conviction that the grace of God thus rendered possible is applicable to our case. But if this is not manifest to us on the evidence of the reality in which we are ourselves placed, it cannot possibly give us the impression of something real.

Owing to its failure to give clear impression to this simple truth, evangelical theology suffered from the start from an indefiniteness which was bound to become an occasion of endless controversy. This is already apparent in the fourth article of the *Augustana*. For when the Reformers there assert with Paul (Rom. iii. 28) that man is justified by faith, and then explain the *per fidem* by the following words: *cum credunt se in gratiam recipi propter Christum, qui sua morte pro peccatis nostris satisfecit* ("when they believe themselves received into grace for Christ's sake who by his death made satisfaction for our sins"), this is very far from securing a definite understanding of what justification by faith means. For these words may be and often have been understood to mean that the sinner receives forgiveness if he accepts the doctrine of the reconciling work of Christ. It can, indeed, be said that this explanation is excluded in the same article by the explanation that men are not justified by their own works and efforts; for this implies that assent to a doctrine which rises from their own choice cannot help them. According to this explanation the words *cum credunt se in gratiam recipi propter Christum* can only mean that sinners are justified if the confidence arises in them that God in his working upon them through Christ and Christ's work enables them to receive the forgiveness of their sins. Obviously in that case the

faith which can so conceive of Christ and his work is
not a condition which must be fulfilled by us in order
that we may receive God's forgiveness; but this faith
is the form in which the sinner experiences forgiveness
as his re-acceptance into fellowship with God.   That
this is the original sense of the Reformers' doctrine of
justification is to be seen from the manner in which
the Apology of the *Augustana* develops the formula
that the sinner is not justified *propter fidem* but *per
fidem.*   According to this, faith must not be distinguished as a work of human effort from the salvation
which is the work of God; but faith as the trust in God
wrought in us through the power of Jesus is itself
salvation.   This is not contradicted by the fact that
faith so understood as God's new creation is at the
same time described by the Reformers as the true
obedience to God, as absolute devotion to him—as, that
is to say, a truly free work of man.   It is precisely in
this combination of both ideas in the concept of faith
that we find for the first time a right understanding of
the concept of religion.

### 52. *The eternal election of the faithful.*

That the believer knows himself to be eternally
elected by God is indicated by Paul (Rom. viii. 28–30).
The following considerations make clear why faith
expresses in this knowledge its assurance of salvation:
1. If God's thoughts towards us are really those of a
Father, it follows that we are a part of the purpose of
his own existence.   We are included, therefore, in the
eternal goal of his working.   2. He who can honestly
say that all things serve his highest good implies that

everything which was and is real in time and space exists for his sake.  He distinguishes from the world, therefore, as the final goal that for which he himself is destined—what God would make of him.  If, then, we are unable to recognize ourselves as eternally elected by God, either we have no faith at all, or else we have not attained to any clear understanding of the real implications of our faith.  On the other hand, the doctrine of a double predestination which, following Rom. ix–xi, Luther and Calvin developed even more crudely than Augustine, has no basis in faith, but is an attempt to solve a problem which does not arise from faith and for which faith has no solution.

But the fact that the Bible contains such a development of thought as we find pre-eminently in Rom. ix. 20–23 should also subserve our salvation, if it brings us to face the question whether we are prepared to follow Scripture even in that which we cannot understand to be a notion rooted in our faith.  If we decide to do this, we are treating the Bible as a law-book which requires from us external obedience.  This is what the Roman Church does.  This is its loyalty to Scripture. But in reality this marks a falling away from the fundamental idea of Scripture; for a faith that repudiates such a law is thereby denied to be faith.  There could be no crasser misuse of Scripture than this! for Scripture was given us for the awakening of faith, and so only is it a means to our salvation.

## 53. *The hope which faith inspires.*

If Jesus' disciples as a result of that experience of God's rule which Christ has brought them—in their faith, that is to say—think of God with joy and desire, this gives rise to the hope that God will one day take away out of their lives everything that in this life can separate them from him (1 Cor. xv. 28; 2 Cor. v. 1–8; Rom. viii. 23).   But faith can only cherish this hope because at the same time one vital element of faith is the will to do battle against everything that hinders amongst men a fellowship of free beings, that fellowship of love in which alone God's rule can be fully realized.   If the hope of a new world beyond this does not definitely include this idea and is not bound up with this will, it is devotion not to God but to the earthly, and consequently it is entirely lacking in the characteristic quality of faith.   We look for the complete possession of that which makes us blessed solely in virtue of personal union with the Spirit, the traces of whose working in history possess the power of saving our present life from utter futility.   This is why Paul longs to find his home in Christ (2 Cor. v. 8).   But there is truth in such a longing only when, as in the case of the apostle in Phil. i. 23, it is associated with the will to serve the brethren in this world as long as possible; for only as we thus make ourselves instruments of the will of Jesus is our longing to be with him genuine.

## SECTION III

### CHAPTER X

## GOD'S PRESENCE IN THE HISTORICAL FACTORS OF REDEMPTION

54. *The religious knowledge of the Divinity of Christ.*

If through our experience of Jesus' power we know ourselves to be again united to God or reconciled to him, then the redemption which we have thus received opens out into thoughts which lead the Christian to a new understanding of the reality in which he lives, and thus to the possession of a new inner life. As a result we find particularly in our daily experiences ever new and surprising manifestations of God's care for us. But we also reach the point at which we recognize one Almighty God in the power of the Person of Jesus that works upon us. This happens for the following reasons :—

1. He who knows himself to have been brought by the power of the Person of Jesus to real trust in God is indubitably led to form the idea that in the working of Jesus upon him the will that rules in the life of God is unveiled. But the life of God cannot become manifest to us except only as he himself allows us to feel

after and find him (Acts xvii. 27). Hence, if Jesus overcomes in us all our uncertainty about God's reality and about his attitude to us, he thereby produces in us the thought that the personal Spirit who presses upon us and reveals himself to us in the working of Jesus is none other than God himself (John xiv. 9).

2. The man who is inwardly overcome by the power of the Person of Jesus experiences in this same inner transaction God's forgiveness of his sins (cf. §48). But beyond question we can only possess God's forgiveness provided God himself gives us experience of the fact that we are dear to him and that in spite of our sins he is seeking fellowship with us. Therefore Jesus' power to assure us of God's forgiveness makes us also realize that in this working of Jesus upon us we have met with the personal God himself (Mark ii. 7; 2 Cor. v. 19; Rom. viii. 39).

3. As soon as Jesus has in this way become for us the pledge of God's love we are inevitably bound to think of him as a living presence. Then he becomes to us, though hidden from us now, the very power of the love that saves sinners. But this power that encompasses us is our God.

In a famous statement in his *Loci* (1521) Melanchthon said that it is in this way that we recognize Jesus Christ as that which he really is—recognize him, that is to say, in his divinity. Ten years later he repeated the statement in the Apology of the *Augustana*, II. §§76 and 101, and III. §§182 and 277. We may with Luther express this knowledge of Christ's divinity by saying that when we feel Jesus' power over our souls we look into God's heart. On the other hand, however,

the redemption through Christ is only consummated
in us, and secured in its religious sense, when our
experience of his working upon us issues in the conception of his divinity.  For the fundamental experience of all true religion that God alone is the Redeemer
must not be submerged by the fact that Christ redeems
us; rather is it in this very fact that it must be clear
for all to see.  Thus Christian faith can only remain
pure religion as the conception of Christ's divinity
arises in it in its truly religious sense.

The more God becomes to us a reality of experience
the more we realize God's rule in us which alone can
redeem us.  But the effect Jesus has upon us is that
in his working we are bound to see God himself turning
to us and ready to save us.  Whoever has this experience in connection with the Person of Christ will find
growing within him this thought of Christ's divinity.
Rightly understood this thought is simply a full expression of the Christian faith in God.  The thought of
Christ's divinity, therefore, in so far as it really belongs
to the life of faith has the following meaning: the
Person of Christ gives to us what only God himself
can give, and is to us what only God himself can be.
In Jesus, therefore, we have before us not simply an
isolated manifestation of God, such as we find in every
other experience religiously interpreted, but the revelation of God, which first makes a religious experience
fully possible to us and secures us in it; or, as Paul
expresses it in Col. ii. 9, we have the complete fullness
of the One Personal God.  Absolutely nothing else
about God can be manifest to us save only his working
directed at ourselves.  But this is unveiled before us

in full clearness in our experience of the Person of Jesus as we see it. In the thought of Christ's divinity, therefore, faith gives expression to a marvellous fact which it finds confronting it.

But if this is what we find in Christ, we confess too that he stands in a relation to God different from that of any other man. We have no terms in which we can adequately express this relationship of Jesus to God. We can only represent it by the Biblical expression offered us in the New Testament, Son of God (John i. 14; Rom. viii. 32). Every attempt to solve this mystery of the Person of Jesus has only led to forumlæ which no one can understand. They are all also from the outset radically at variance with the declaration of Jesus, preserved for us in Matt. xi. 27, that a knowledge which should unveil the mystery of his Person must remain for us unattainable, since only God himself perfectly knows him. When the thought of Christ's divinity arises in those men who alone are capable of grasping it—in those, that is to say, who have found through him the completely convincing revelation and the forgiveness of God (1 Cor. xii. 3), they will henceforth adopt that form of the preaching of redemption through Christ which we meet with in Paul: they will henceforward say that God has redeemed them by the blood of His Son. But this can only be true for the man who knows Jesus and has experienced in him the redeeming power of God.

## 55. *The Christological dogma.*

The religious recognition of Christ's divinity constitutes the chief content of the Gospel of John. Further expression was also given to this genuinely religious recognition at the first œcumenical synod of Nicea. For the formula ομοουσιος τω πατρι does not mean that the Son is of like nature with the Father. It expresses something much greater, namely, that he is of the same nature as the Father. This means that our faith sees in Jesus Christ no less than in the Father the one personal Spirit who alone is God. But at that time it was no longer clearly seen how Christians arrive at this recognition. Therefore the old Catholic theology made no attempt to indicate the union of God and man in Christ as a fact visible to faith, but tried to conceive of its possibility, in order at least in this way to lend confirmation to the idea. But this is bound to lead to the loss of the religious conception. For that conception points to a fact which is grasped in the faith of those whom Christ has redeemed, but which at the same time is clearly seen by such to be incomprehensible. Instead of this, men now gave themselves up to a conception which is entirely destitute of religious significance, since it is inconsistent with monotheism. For to make God's incarnation in Christ intelligible, two possible alternatives were open. Some supposed the divine nature in Christ to be some kind of demi-god for whom a union with human nature was possible. In this case, while God himself cannot become man, this is possible for the Son or λογος, who is distinguished from God and is not αυτοθεος, yet still united to him. Others understood by the Godhead a kind of deity who could include in himself a number of individuals. Both roads led back to the polytheism which men in their controversy with the Arians had sought to avoid by the Nicene formula. All these attempts were highly dangerous to the clarity of the Christian faith. In order to make God's incarnation intelligible men either refused, like Apollinaris of Laodicea, to recognize the full reality of the human nature in Christ, or else like Arius they substituted for the presence of God in the personal life and working of Jesus the union of the man Jesus with a kind of demi-god, or they simply abandoned the idea of a real union of God and man in Christ and contented themselves like Nestorius with a mere collocation of the two.

All these aberrations of Christological speculation were to have been cut away by the formula of the Council of Chalcedon. For it was there declared that the Lord in whom the Church believes is the λογος, become man in Christ, who is to be regarded as the common meeting-point of the two natures, the divine and the human, which are in him indissolubly united while remaining unimpaired in their essential characteristics. This Chalcedonian dogma, then, declared that the Church would condone no Christological speculation which did not give full recognition to the divinity of Christ and to his humanity, and to the unity of his Person in the possession of both natures. This, indeed, meant the abandonment of the Nicene conception—the correct conception—of the way in which the divinity of Christ could be understood in a religious sense. It was no longer considered that the Christian community can only call Christ its Lord so long as it can see at work in him the one eternal God, and that it will not do to seek to base Christian faith upon the hypothesis that in Christ divine nature is united with human nature. The fact that at that time satisfaction could be felt with this conception is bound up with that vague idea of redemption which as early as Irenæus had driven off the field the Pauline and Johannine recognition of the manner of our redemption through Christ. It had been forgotten, therefore, that Christian faith, if it treats Christ as God, must have before its eyes, without being able to comprehend it, a wonderful fact which it recognizes as the source and the foundation of its own life.

The Reformers, indeed, regained this recognition, but they did not fully work it out. Luther at least wanted to set aside as unsatisfactory the conception of the Chalcedonian dogma that in Christ divine and human nature were joined because they met in a common subject, the Logos. For he had recovered the recognition that in the power of the Man Jesus over us we apprehend God himself working upon us. The conclusion ought, indeed, to have been drawn that the terms of that early Church Christology should be generally abandoned. For it would no longer be satisfactory to speak of a divine *nature,* subsisting beneath the human life of Jesus. For in this way neither was satisfaction found for a need of salvation which God himself desires to see operative in the individual life, nor could those ideas provide expression for the consciousness of the fact that the Christian sees God working upon him in the power of Jesus over his soul. This Christology of the early Church corresponds with the conception of redemption current at the time, that human nature has the powers of the divine nature bestowed upon it. On the other hand, as soon as men came to share Luther's understanding of redemption as the sinner's experience of inward reconciliation with God, the old Christology had to be replaced by giving a clear indication of the way in which we are able, through the power of the Person of Jesus upon us, to find the God who in spite of our sins is seeking fellowship with us. But Luther continued to employ the inadequate notion of a divine nature in Christ. All he did was to introduce a modification of the Christology of the Early Church, and in this he was followed by the Lutheran orthodoxy according to the terms of the Formula of Concord, while the Reformed theology chose to stand by the dogma of Chalcedon.

But in this Lutheran doctrine not only, as hitherto, was a *unio personalis* of the natures affirmed, but a direct union of both or a *communio naturarum*. As a result of this a *communicatio idiomatum* was taught, meaning not any communication of human attributes to the divine nature, but the communication of the *efficacious* attributes of the divine nature to the human.

It is to be recognized that in this doctrine, too, there is really an attempt to express our experience of the Person of Jesus—namely that, when its spell falls upon us, we feel we are in the presence of God himself; but it immediately became apparent that this new knowledge was the very thing that could not be expressed in any mere modification of the early Church Christology. For it was no longer possible to hold firmly to the reality of the human life of Jesus if the idea of the union of the two natures had been carried to the point where the human was endowed with the divine attributes of omnipotence and omniscience. For this reason the Lutherans found themselves driven to the doctrine that Christ's human nature during its life on earth had emptied itself not indeed of the possession, but of the use of its divine attributes (the orthodox *kenosis* doctrine). But here, quite apart from other purely logical inconsistencies, we are back at the view which Luther found religiously unsatisfactory in the early Church dogma, that God himself is not to be apprehended in the earthly life of Jesus, but is only to be assumed as standing in the background. This fault, then, is still further enhanced in the *kenosis* doctrine of modern Lutherans. For it is here maintained that the Second Person of the Godhead, namely, God himself in his incarnation, emptied himself not only of the use but also of the possession of a part of his divine attributes, or that he sank into some kind of unconscious life. It was such ideas as these of the modern Lutherans that the authors of the Formula of Concord had in mind. But at that time they condemned it as an error destructive of the Christian faith (*Epitome,* Ch. viii. §39). Beyond doubt a Being in whom God was only latent and not apparent to us would not have been able to redeem us in our inward life. It is no less certain that we abandon the Biblical view of God if we suppose that he could lay aside one of his attributes, or that at one time he did lay aside some of them. Such a conception is no longer an expression of real religion but a capricious work of phantasy. The texts of Scripture, however, to which this last form of Christological speculation appeals, Phil. ii. 5–11 in particular, are not susceptible of this interpretation. They assert, indeed, that during his earthly life Christ found himself in a situation which did not correspond with his nature and to which he had submitted on our behalf, so that he became thereby an example for his disciples. But in the first place we can no longer determine what Paul understood by the pre-existent Christ. All that is clear is that by this he cannot have meant God himself. In the second place those passages do not assert that we cannot now apprehend Almighty God in the Man Jesus because God was only latent in him and thus does not meet us in a way that we can apprehend. If that had been the significance of Paul's words about a κένωσις, not only would they be inconsistent with the fundamental idea of the Johannine Gospel, but further, in these words Paul would be going back upon what he says himself in Rom. v. 15; viii. 39; and 2 Cor. v. 19 as to the ground of the assurance of salvation in the Christian community.

56. *God in the life of redeemed men* (*the Holy Spirit*).

Paul presupposes that all Christians have received God's Spirit (Gal. iii. 2). Even where he sternly reproves Christians, he reminds them that God's Spirit dwells in them (1 Cor. iii. 16; vi. 19): "Know ye not that ye are a temple of God?" But he demands from them, too, that they should know this possession by its fruits. Whoever has not this Spirit does not belong to Christ (Rom. viii. 9). Whoever, therefore, did not know from his own experience that he had received God's Spirit, and how the Spirit works in him, could not regard himself as redeemed (1 John iii. 24).

This Spirit is called God's Spirit and Christ's Spirit. In distinction from the natural life of the spirit it is the life-producing power (1 Cor. xv. 45).

But if we ask how the assurance of this possession grows up in us, Paul points us not to outward things such as the laying on of hands or anointing, but to the faith which Christ has created in us. This also gives us a clear idea of the nature of the Spirit which Paul in Rom. viii. 9 calls God's Spirit and immediately afterwards Christ's Spirit.

1. In our faith we are conscious of the fact that the depths of the godhead are made accessible for us. For without this conviction faith would not imply a confidence more perfect than any we could put in men. Now the innermost essence of personal life lies perfectly open only to its own consciousness. If in the last resort the human personality remains to everyone else an inscrutable mystery, this applies in the highest degree to the personal God. Hence, if in spite of this there is produced in us a faith which is conscious of knowing the depths of the Deity, this faith must also give birth to the thought that in these spiritual motions of its own it can recognize the thinking, that is the life, of the very Spirit of God. Thus Paul expounds the idea of the Holy Ghost in 1 Cor. ii. He says in verse 12 that we received the Spirit from God that we might be assured of what is freely given to us by God's grace.

2. In our faith we possess the knowledge that in Jesus and in his work on us God is realizing his eternal purpose. By him were all things created, in the heavens and on earth, things visible and things in-

visible; through him and for him were all things created (Col. i. 16). It follows that what the revelation of God's love in Christ works in us, sincere devotion to God, means God's own realizing of the life which he desires for himself eternally. Since, however, Almighty God realizes through his own action this purpose of his to rule over us through Christ, we are bound to see in the motions of faith within us motions of God's Spirit in which he aims at his eternal goal. Thus the believer's own assurance of sonship of God, which expresses itself in the prayer of perfect trust, reveals itself to him as the life of God's Spirit within him (Rom. viii. 16; Gal. iv. 6).

3. The truth of the idea that God's Spirit works in us is confirmed by that which faith makes of us. From the beginning the motions of faith in us are opposed to flesh and blood (Matt. xvi. 17). If the thoughts of faith become powerful in us we experience this necessarily as the victory of supernatural powers, because these thoughts always involve a break with the way of thinking which is natural to man in virtue of his dependence on the world. The natural man receiveth not the things of the Spirit of God, for they are foolishness to him; he cannot understand them (1 Cor. ii. 14). The Spirit from God which brings us into opposition with the way of thinking of the natural life is Holy Spirit. He who cannot know anything of such experiences cannot be a Christian. If we do not perceive in ourselves anything of the struggle of the spirit against the flesh (Gal. v. 17), if we do not feel the unrest which presses on beyond all that we have hitherto attained, towards an eternal goal (Phil. iii.

12–14), but instead feel satisfied with our present attainments (1 Cor. iv. 8), we are in danger of losing God's Spirit.

From all this, we can also infer what is in the last resort the anchorage of our assurance that the super-natural power of God's Spirit is working in us. We may continue to draw support from this thought, just so long as we are still alive to the fact that we can never again forget Jesus Christ, since we feel ourselves united with him by the power of his Spirit. Here lies the root of faith, the life of which in man means the possession of God's Spirit. This possession is identical with the rule of Christ living and present in his own. (2 Cor. iii. 17).

The briefest expression for the nature of the Holy Spirit is this: God in us and Christ in us. The question, therefore, whether the Holy Spirit is to be thought of as personally living or as impersonal force indicates a complete failure to understand these conceptions of faith. The Holy Spirit is simply the living God present and working in us.

### 57. *God in the community of the believers* (*the Church of Faith.*)

The birth of faith and its driving power tend to bind Christians together; for it is by personal life domin-ated by God's Spirit that the rise of faith is mediated in every individual case. But the faith that exists in us constrains us to enter into fellowship with others who can likewise say of themselves that they have been brought to God by Christ; for to have com-munion with believers is necessary to the life of faith, necessary because such communion issues in an enriched conception of the fact to which it owes its life. The fellowship thus arising Paul calls the community of God or of Christ, the ἐκκλησία. The saving significance of this fellowship in the case of every individual faith seems to lie in the fact that the exalted Christ is present in it as the guiding spiritual power or as its Head (John xiv. 16–21; Eph. iii. 21; v. 23–32) and makes it a dwelling-place of God (1 Tim. iii. 15). The spiritual life to be found in this fellowship throws open in the midst of mankind the approach to the grace of God manifested in Christ (Matt. xvi. 19; xviii. 18). Here is made available for sinful men a place where the good may grow, because here everything that elsewhere sunders men from one another can be overcome (Eph. ii. 14–18; Gal. iii. 28). Whoever has had experience of the Christian community in this its true significance, and yet separates himself from it, is lost. But since Christ is present in the daily communion of every gathering of Christians, however small (Matt. xviii. 20), every such gathering represents the whole ἐκκλησία (Rom. xvi. 6; 1 Cor. xvi. 19; Col. iv. 15; Philem. v. 2).

This Christian conception of the fellowship of the saints and of its significance for salvation is distorted when, as in Catholicism, the possession of the Holy Spirit and the power to impart it is ascribed to the officials of the duly organized Church. These officials, and the ecclesiastical organization that accompanies them, do not represent that Church or community of the Lord of the reality of which we are convinced by faith, and which always remains the same; they are simply instruments developed and employed by believers in different ways at different times.

That the fellowship which confesses Christ is really a fellowship of believers is to *us* guaranteed by the fact that we see operative in it that means of salvation by which faith knows itself to have been created. By this is meant everything which brings near to a man the revelation of God in Christ or the word of God. Every man we meet who experiences inward emancipation through God is God's word to us. But this significance attaches in a pre-eminent degree to the expression of faith which we find in unequalled measure in Holy Scripture. The evangelical Churches, however, associate with the word of God as means of salvation also baptism and the Lord's Supper. In elucidation of them we find the following in the confessional writings of both evangelical Churches:—

First, these symbolic actions can have a significance for salvation only in so far as they are understood by the recipient as God's message to him, that is to say, in so far as they are modes of the Word. Whoever cannot apprehend and grasp them as words of God, cannot find in them a means of grace (*Confessio Augustana,* Art. XIII.; Apology of the Augsburg Confession, Ch. vii. § 5).

In the second place God does not reveal himself in these actions in such a way as to create faith by means of them. Rather does he thereby bestow comfort on a faith which is already there (Apol. vii. § 20). This is the meaning we must give to the name μυστήριον or *sacramentum.* The saving significance of these actions is entirely hidden from the unbeliever. To him, therefore, they inevitably appear worthless, or, if he ascribes any value to them, he regards them as a magical agency. The believer, on the other hand, should be in a position to receive the *sacramentum* offered him in such a way as to be able to find in it a word of God's grace specially addressed to him (Apol., vii. §§ 21–22).

## 58. *The doctrine of the Trinity.*

The doctrine of the Trinity rightly understood is an expression of monotheism in its final form. It is involved in the revelation, to which our faith consciously owes its life, that we can perfectly picture to ourselves the God who redeems us only in three aspects. He is to us the Father to whom we may appeal with the confidence of being heard. He is similarly Jesus' spiritual power working upon us. But he is to us also the Spirit who overcomes the overwhelming might of nature both in ourselves and in the fellowship of believers. The doctrine of the Trinity must always start from the fact that God reveals to us his single Nature in this threefold way (economical Trinity).

But the theology of the Church has rightly advanced from this to the thought that it must be essentially involved in God's nature to reveal himself in this threefold way. On the other hand, the attempts to comprehend the necessity of this threefold revelation of the One God have from the time of Augustine up till the present rather obscured than elucidated the thought of the Trinity. Augustine himself virtually admitted the futility of such attempts when he explained that "person" when used of the Trinity means something different from "person" when used elsewhere. The word does not indicate three divine personalities. What it does indicate in positive terms neither he nor anyone after him has ever been able to say. His doctrine of the Trinity is expressed in the so-called *Symbolum Athanasianum* in the words *in hoc trinitate nihil prius aut posterius, nihil maius aut minus, sed totæ personæ coæternæ sibi sunt et coæquales.* The Church, too, has always cherished the intention to follow this conception of Augustine's; but the danger that the doctrine of the Trinity might lead to a dissolution of monotheism has not always been avoided.

The doctrine of the Trinity reminds us that we can only find eternal life in fellowship with God if he remains unsearchable to us—an eternal mystery. The way to the Christian religion is the unconditioned will to truth or to submission to the facts which we ourselves experience. But its beginning and its end is, none the less, the humbling of man before the Unsearchable. "God dwelleth in light unapproachable, whom no man hath seen, nor can see" (1 Tim. vi. 16).

www.ingramcontent.com/pod-product-compliance
Lightning Source LLC
Chambersburg PA
CBHW060352090426
42734CB00011B/2117